MEN OF INTELLIGENCE

Major-General
Sir Kenneth Strong K.B.E., C.B.

MEN OF INTELLIGENCE

A Study of the Roles and Decisions of
Chiefs of Intelligence from World War I
to the present day

A GINIGER BOOK
published in association with
CASSELL · LONDON

CASSELL & COMPANY LTD
35 Red Lion Square, London, WC1
Melbourne, Sydney, Toronto
Johannesburg, Auckland

A Giniger Book
Copyright © 1970 by Major-General Sir Kenneth Strong
First published 1970

UB
250
S66

I.S.B.N. 0 304 93652 9

Printed in Great Britain by
The Camelot Press Ltd
London and Southampton

F. 770

THIS BOOK IS DEDICATED TO THE
MEN OF INTELLIGENCE
WHOSE SEARCH FOR BETTER AND MORE ACCURATE
INFORMATION MUST BE CONSTANT AND
UNREMITTING

PREFACE

In my memoir *Intelligence at the Top* I attempted to describe my experiences as an Intelligence officer during the past forty years or more, and to outline some of the lessons that seemed to stem from these experiences. It is my hope that descriptions of some of the individuals who have played important parts in the Intelligence structures of their countries in peace and war will help to spread a broader understanding of the true nature of Intelligence and its sources and operations. None of the individuals I mention would lay any claim to have been an elusive 'master spy'; rarely would any of them have wished to disguise his identity; only very occasionally, if ever, would any of them have carried a concealed pistol. Intelligence, as I shall have occasion to repeat many times in the course of this book, is not primarily a matter of secret operations and secret sources; it is instead a matter of judgement and evaluation, and it is in this field of evaluation and so-called 'estimating' that men of Intelligence have played their most decisive roles. They are diverse in characters and aptitudes; one characteristic they all share, however, is that they have spent large parts of their working lives attempting to arrive at solutions to difficult and complicated problems on the basis of incomplete knowledge, and, what is more, aware that inaccurate or ill-considered answers may cost lives.

Many of the principal characters in this book were known to me personally. By nationality they are German, French, British and American, and their lives in Intelligence together cover the period from the beginning of World War I until 1965. In 1914, for example, Lieutenant-Colonel Hentsch, the chief Intelligence officer on the staff of General von Moltke, Chief of the German General Staff, came almost by accident to be at least partly responsible for the eventual German defeat in World War I. Colonel Walther Nicolai was the Chief of the German Secret Service throughout the whole of that war. On the British side, General Charteris, until his dismissal chief Intelligence officer to the British Commander-in-Chief, General Sir Douglas Haig (later Field-Marshal Lord Haig), played an important, if somewhat disquieting, part in the later stages of that war.

Between the wars, French Intelligence watched with apprehension the resurrection of German armed might. General Gauché, the head of the Deuxième Bureau, was the principal French Intelligence officer concerned with estimating German strength, and his activities and extraordinarily accurate analyses are of considerable interest in the history of the period. General Didelet, the French military attaché in Berlin, was one of the few of the Western community in Berlin in the years immediately before World War II whose estimates were sometimes badly misleading.

On the German side during the same period, Colonel Ulrich Liss was responsible at German Army High Command for estimates of the French, British and American forces. Most of his analyses also were brilliantly accurate. As far as German estimates of Russia were concerned, I have felt it useful to include some comments upon General Kurt von Tippelskirch, who held a position which corresponded approximately to Director of Military Intelligence at the War Office in London. Finally, no remarks on German Intelligence between the wars and during World War II could be complete without at least passing references to Admiral Canaris, the head of the Secret Service (the 'Abwehr') of the German Supreme Command, and to General Gehlen who later became the chief of the West German Government's most secret Intelligence organization.

To represent Britain and the United States I have chosen three men. The first is Bill Cavendish-Bentinck, who from 1939 to 1945 was responsible for the co-ordination of British Intelligence efforts and for the provision to the British Government of joint Intelligence estimates. He was the first 'Director' of Intelligence in the sense in which we now employ the term, and his position represented the beginnings of the system which was later developed with enormous success in the United States.

For it was in the United States, after the war, that Intelligence really came into its own, and a true school of professionals emerged. From an embarrassment of American choice I have selected two Directors of Central Intelligence—Allen Dulles and John A. McCone. The former represents an era in which the operator and the estimator were combined; with his resignation after the Bay of Pigs episode during the Kennedy administration a colourful chapter in the history of Intelligence was closed. McCone on the other hand represents new thinking about the role of Intelligence in national policy- and decision-making in an era of increasingly technological sources and increasingly complex problems.

In addition, I have taken the opportunity offered by this book to comment on three other subjects. I have included brief chapters on Intelligence and armistices and on the relevance and importance of spies, and I have concluded with some additional thoughts on the relationship of Intelligence to decision-making in government and business fields.

Once again I must acknowledge the help I have received from many sources. First, I am most grateful to Sir John Wheeler-Bennett and Major-General Sir Maurice Dowse; without their help and encouragement I am doubtful if this book would have been started, let alone finished. Secondly, I must thank Brigadier van Cutsem, my chief at the beginning of World War II; Major-General F. G. Beaumont-Nesbitt, the British Director of Military Intelligence in 1939; Mr Donald McLachlan; Mr D. W. King, the Chief Librarian and his staff at the Ministry of Defence for much trouble taken on my behalf; General Sir James Marshall-Cornwall, who kindly allowed me to read some of his private papers; Brigadier C. T. Edwards and Mr Martin Watson, both of whom are knowledgeable about Intelligence matters; the late Captain Sir Basil Liddell Hart for his information about Haig and Charteris; Frau Erika Liss for photographs and details of her husband's life; the staff of the Imperial War Museum for their help; and finally my old friend Ted Weintal, formerly of *Newsweek* magazine. Thirdly, I am most glad of the opportunity to pay a tribute, albeit carefully censored, to the work of Bill Cavendish-Bentinck, and I must thank him for permitting this. I am grateful for the assistance of Alan Crick, Edward Thomas and Jack Trotman, whose combined theoretical and practical experience of Intelligence is wide. I am especially indebted to Jack Trotman, who has once again helped me with the preparation of my book for publication. I would also like to thank Kenneth Parker and the other members of Cassell who have shown infinite patience in helping me with this book, and with my first book *Intelligence at the Top*, to negotiate the hurdles in the path of a newcomer to the business of writing books.

I have made free use of the available literature dealing with the subjects and the periods of which I write; in particular, I have relied heavily on the books by Gauché and Liss and have accepted almost without reservation their accounts of the events with which they were concerned. I knew both these men and I heard from their own lips much of what they later recorded in print; I can offer no higher praise than to recommend their works wholeheartedly to students of these subjects. I have listed these books, and others which I found useful, in the bibliography, but if I have at any point failed to make an appropriate acknowledgement to any author or publisher I hope those concerned will accept my apologies.

As usual, I must add that, in spite of the help I have received, I am myself responsible for the judgements in this book and for any errors of fact.

July 1970   K. S.

CONTENTS

ILLUSTRATIONS

INTELLIGENCE

The word 'Intelligence', which has no exact equivalent in either French or German, is used in this book in two senses. First, it is used for the end-product of the process of co-ordination of raw, uncollated and unevaluated information: thus, 'The Intelligence presented to the Commander was faulty'. Secondly, it is used as the name of the structure responsible for producing this end-product: for example, 'Intelligence was well aware of what was happening'.

1

WORLD WAR I

In 1912, at the age of twelve, I went with my parents to spend a long summer in Marburg where my father was a visiting professor. Marburg is an ancient university town beautifully situated on the banks of the tiny River Lahn, and it housed a small German infantry garrison, perhaps a battalion or even a regiment. I do not think I ever knew its name or number—my Intelligence instincts were not then sufficiently developed—but my main joy that summer was to watch the German troops drilling and training on their parade ground. While preparing for our visit to Germany, my father had subscribed to a weekly publication *Die Woche* which often contained pictures of the German armed forces, the officers in their tight-fitting, perfectly-cut uniforms, sometimes sporting monocles, the soldiers goose-stepping, disciplined and unsmiling. I was fascinated, and in Marburg I saw such men in person. Hardly a day passed but I was hanging over one or other of the fences surrounding the barracks, absorbed by the activity and sometimes slightly scared by the apparent brutalities I witnessed. Men who could not scale obstacles with sufficient speed were cussed and dragooned. The many who collapsed at bayonet or rifle drill in the unbearable heat of a really fierce July were carried away as a matter of routine.

My constant interest at last drew the attention of the authorities, and on one of my evening visits I was approached by two of the German non-commissioned officers. They were very friendly and addressed me in English, explaining that they were studying for an examination in the language. What impressed me was the contrast between their behaviour on the parade ground and their personal kindness both to me and to other soldiers who joined us. Sometimes, in the evenings, I would take up a position which gave me a good view of the officers' 'casino', or club. The windows were usually open to the glorious summer nights and I could see the interiors of the rooms, with their fine furnishings. More often than not I could hear the sound of music. Then suddenly one of the monocled figures would emerge from the casino, and make his way to the barrack square, his sword clanking on the ground as he walked. He was presumably a duty officer, making his rounds. 'Der Herr kommt'—'The boss is coming'—went the whisper, and everyone, including myself, stood strictly to attention. I was entranced.

★

Two years later, in 1914, while the clouds were gathering for World War I, General Helmuth Graf von Moltke, the Chief of the Imperial General Staff and thus in effect commander of the field army of Germany, was quietly taking the cure at Karlsbad. Moltke was in his sixties and not in good health; he suffered from a heart ailment with some complications. He had been selected by Kaiser Wilhelm II to succeed Count Schlieffen—of whom more later—largely because he was the nephew of the great Field-Marshal von Moltke, victor of the Austro-Prussian War of 1866 and the Franco-Prussian War of 1870, and had accepted the appointment somewhat reluctantly. In appearance and interests he was somewhat different from the traditional German officer. He was tall and powerfully built rather than slim and elegant; further, he had intellectual pretensions and played the cello as a hobby. While his contemporaries recognized that he was hard-working and competent, many doubted whether he had the determination and strength of character necessary to control Germany's individualistic generals and direct the immense German war machine, and there were general regrets that good men had been thrust aside in the promotion race, while courtiers and sycophants were promoted. Apart from his ill health, Moltke was lucky to be taking the cure. Some of his colleagues at the top of the German military hierarchy had been bidden to attend the Kiel Regatta as the Kaiser's guests; here they were condemned to long and dreary lectures on strategy by experts on the American Civil War. They did, however, have some other diversions not normally met with in conventional military circles. Count Hülser-Haseler, the Chief of the Military Cabinet, was wont to entertain the Kaiser's guests by dressing as a member of a *corps de ballet* and pirouetting in a most professional manner. His career ended only when he fell down dead after one particularly strenuous performance.

It is difficult today to understand the prestige which in pre-1914 days in Europe attached to the German officer corps. A rigid selection process, mainly academic but partly social, ensured that only those officers with unimpeachable qualifications and ability could gain entry to it. They jealously guarded their prerogatives and, immune from the jurisdiction of the civil courts and the police, had their own courts of honour; the punishment they feared most greatly was to be stripped of their uniforms and privileges and to be degraded to mere civilian status. The carmine stripes on the trouser legs and the silver collar badges which some of them displayed were the outward signs of the special position they had attained as members of the Imperial General Staff. The selection procedures and the rigorous training meant that members of the General Staff were a class apart and tended to think and reason on similar lines, and to reach similar—often identical—conclusions on similar military problems. They trusted each others' military judgement implicitly, and felt they could rely on any individual, whatever his rank, making a military appreciation or decision which would be logical and sound and acceptable to all. Thus it sometimes happened that a junior officer who had been accepted into the General Staff was permitted to take decisions of tremendous importance, and entrusted with responsibilities far beyond those normal for his rank. He could give orders in the name of the Chief of the Imperial General Staff; he was no mere messenger but was presumed to be sufficiently in touch with the situation to be able to explain the nature and intentions of the orders which he carried. In any case, he would be generally well known personally to commanders and their principal staff officers, so a general trust was reinforced by a personal confidence.

General Staff training, aimed at producing men of independence and confidence, had its weaknesses. A certain inflexibility of judgement which, somewhat paradoxically, accompanied independence, did not always allow for the unexpected. Von Kluck, the commander of the German First Army at the outset of the war, could not bring himself to believe that the French soldier, after days of exhausting retreat in August and September 1914, was capable of turning at the bugle call and forcing the Germans back to the Marne. Nor did the General Staff believe the British Army was a fighting force to be reckoned with. They failed to appreciate that if the Americans joined the war they would prove effective in combat; a quarter of a century later they made the same error. On both occasions, although they had a reasonable knowledge of American order of battle, equipment and dispositions, they did not understand that the American environment with its massive industrial base, its high standard of living, and its reliance on modern methods could encourage individual qualities of exceptional value on the battlefield. They failed to observe that, in military terms, the Americans were basically obedient. In North Africa and Europe in World War II, for example, Eisenhower had much the same problems of command as did Moltke in 1914. But whereas Eisenhower expected and enforced obedience from his American and his British subordinate army and other commanders, we shall see that Moltke had little influence over the actions of the commanders of his armies.

In order to understand the part which Intelligence played in the vital events at the beginning of World War I, it is important to know something of the German command structure and of German plans at the time. The structure had remained virtually unchanged since 1870. The Chief of the Imperial General Staff was the responsible adviser to the Kaiser on the conduct of the land war. In practice the Army was the largest and most important element of the armed forces and therefore the Chief of Staff was in a key position to advise on such important issues as whether the Fatherland had adequate resources to wage a given war, and the general course that strategy should follow. Neither was he averse to giving advice on the war at sea, especially as the admirals tended to vent ideas on ground strategy and tactics. Final decisions of war and peace lay in the hands of the Kaiser, advised by the Imperial Chancellor, Theobald von Bethmann-Hollweg, who was appointed by the Kaiser and responsible to him. In the clash of personalities which proceeded the outbreak of war in early August, Bethmann-Hollweg was amongst those who welcomed the occasional indications that war in the West was not inevitable, and who attempted at the last moment to prevent the advance of German armies against Belgium and Luxembourg.

Once the decision to go to war was taken, the Kaiser as Supreme War Lord exercised command over all his forces. Again there was a considerable difference between theory and practice for in fact this command could only be nominal, especially when the Chief of the Imperial General Staff was an able and determined individual. Nevertheless, the latter did not have the field entirely to himself. The Kaiser's military cabinet handled all officers' promotions, although the Chief of Staff had the final decision concerning the employment of members of the great General Staff. The Secretary of State for War in 1914, General Erich von Falkenhayn, who succeeded Moltke when he failed, was a complicating factor. He held the purse strings and, under the curious German combination of absolute government and so-called popular democracy, was responsible to the German parliament. Falkenhayn, in fact, did not always see eye to eye with the General Staff, although he was a graduate of that body.

This complex system had worked fairly well for the Germans in 1870, although even then the more perceptive German officers had detected flaws in the procedures. It was clear that the almost unlimited freedom possessed by high commanders in the conduct of their operations had on occasion led to some appalling mistakes. But the war was successful, and in the euphoria over the defeat of France apparently small procedural blemishes were soon forgotten. The Germans had never really considered whether their theories and techniques would be adequate to withstand more formidable opposition forty years later.

As Germany's ultimatum to Russia to cease mobilization expired on 1 August 1914, the situation appeared reasonably hopeful to the Germans. Most were convinced that even if the worst happened and Germany was faced with a two-front war, Britain would remain neutral and not come to the assistance of France. Grand Admiral von Tirpitz, the Naval Secretary, did not believe that Britain felt herself threatened. In his view the German fleet need not necessarily be stronger than the British to deter the latter from entering the war; it need only be just strong enough to present Britain with a choice of risks. Much the same concept holds good today in Soviet–American military relations. Moreover, in spite of all logic, nearly everyone was convinced that the war would be short. No economy, it was said, was capable of supporting the demands of modern war for very long. All the parties to the conflict shared this illusion: the British hoped to be 'home by Christmas'.

*

At this most critical time in German history, Colonel Walther Nicolai was Chief of the German Secret Service or Gruppe IIIb of the Imperial General Staff, and to him fell the duty of informing Moltke of what was happening in those countries with which Germany might soon be at war. Nicolai was an unusual German officer. A Prussian, and a member of the General Staff, he had a much wider knowledge of world affairs than most of his contemporaries, and he spoke several languages including Russian, French and Japanese. During his three years at the Staff College from 1901 to 1903, he had been disappointed to find that political matters were seldom discussed, but he must have shown some talent for Intelligence because his first job on leaving the College was to map a fortified area near the River Vistula. He was appointed Chief of the Secret Service of the Imperial General Staff while still a junior major in 1913, and he never ceased to complain that his rank did not give him the necessary authority. On taking over, he was apparently surprised to find that the spies whose activities he had to direct were not always persons of inferior education and social standing, but were frequently strong patriots, men and women of the world, cultivated and politically conscious. This was a source of gratification to him, for he was firmly convinced that work in a secret service must be an 'occupation for gentlemen'. Only they could command obedience from the motley collection of agents and informants on whom he must rely. Good agents, Nicolai wryly commented, wore themselves out quickly; bad agents lived long because they avoided the dangers of their profession.

Nicolai was responsible not only for obtaining information about potential enemies, but also for counter-intelligence—that is to say, combating the attempts of foreign governments to penetrate the military secrets of Germany. The two most important potential enemies Nicolai had to face were Russia and France. He attributed to French Intelligence many sources of information which it probably never possessed, and strong government support, which it certainly did. The French, he believed, had had informants in the German Army since 1894 and were in frequent receipt of information from German deserters right up till the outbreak of war in 1914, many having fled to France to escape the harsh discipline of the German forces. But Nicolai claimed to have concealed two important military facts from them. Firstly, he had prevented anyone knowing that Germany would make use of reserve divisions as first line troops; secondly he had prevented anything becoming known of the enormous new German siege guns.

The Russian Intelligence service had only recently, since the end of the war against Japan, turned its attention to Germany, and Nicolai believed that France, fearing the coming war and attempting to acquire all possible support, was furnishing funds and advice to the Russians to assist the latter's Intelligence operations against Germany.

Nicolai was convinced that Russia had been skilful enough to obtain complete information concerning German plans for the coming campaigns in the East and the West and had passed these to Paris, where they had apparently received less credence than they deserved; the French authorities refused to believe that the Germans would employ such slender forces as the plans revealed for their initial resistance to Russian attacks. Nicolai was never able to prove these points, but material captured from the Russians by the Germans at the Battle of Tannenburg in August 1914, where Hindenburg and Luden-dorff routed the Russian Army under Samsonov and took over 100,000 prisoners, made it clear that the Russian high command was provided with better topographical and industrial material concerning Germany as a theatre of war than was in the possession of the Germans themselves. Later, when the German armies captured Warsaw, they found amongst the Russian records more than a hundred secret German and Austrian official military documents.

Ideology had not yet become a motive behind Russian espionage, which in these years was conducted on a strictly business basis. Their agents were paid in cash and at so much a head for every deserter they induced to defect. Their standards of probity were high. A Russian agent returned from an espionage mission with several deserters to whom he had acted as a guide. As the promised reward was about to be paid to him, he declared that he did not want it. 'These gentlemen', he said, indicating the German deserters, 'have already paid for the privilege.'

Although Nicolai was mainly preoccupied with France and Russia, and continued to be so until after the outbreak of World War I, there were two other areas which caused him some concern before 1914. The first was the activities of the British, whom Nicolai believed to be seeking information about the German and Danish coasts and investiga-ting the Kiel creeks and even the Kiel Canal itself. Clearly a big exten-sion of counter-intelligence operations against Britain would be imperative in the long run.

The second area involved Germany's ostensible allies, Austria-Hungary and Italy. Each of these powers devoted considerable effort to discovering the secrets of the others, and, try as he might, Nicolai was unable to divorce either from this annoying and time-consuming battle of wits, which prevented the emergence of any serious joint and international Intelligence service on the German side during World War I.

In July 1914 Nicolai, who had been enjoying the pleasures of the famous Kiel Week, was holidaying with his family in the Hartz mountains in Germany. The murder of the heir to the Austrian throne and his consort by a Serbian student in Sarajevo in July had earlier led to an international crisis, and reports that Russian forces were mobilizing had been denied in Moscow. In Germany the military routine was unchanged and preparations continued for the army corps manœuvres in the Rhineland. In any case, Nicolai was fairly content. The dispositions of the French and Russian armies, their armaments, their state of training and their fortress systems were all thought to be known, and Nicolai felt he could take credit from the fact that much of the information on which German estimates of the situation were based had originated from his own efforts.

On 25 July 1914 Moltke summoned Nicolai to Berlin. Nicolai did not expect to be away from his wife and family for more than a few days, but the Hartz mountains did not see him again that summer. Two days later, on Monday the 27th, the Kaiser returned to the Prussian capital, having become sufficiently alarmed to forgo the lectures on the American Civil War and curtail a cruise he was taking in Norwegian waters on the royal yacht *Hohenzollern*. This was a busy day for Nicolai, for Moltke had to report personally to the Kaiser with the latest information. In the great Marble Room of the Royal Palace, the Kaiser was informed that the Russian armies were on the move, and that preliminary military precautions were in force in France.

As the hours and days passed, news from both France and Russia continued ominous, and the concensus of reports from all manner of sources was that war on two fronts was likely. On 31 July an agent on the Russian frontier reported that Russia was now fully mobilized, but before Moltke telephoned the Kaiser the agent had to give his word of honour that the information he was giving was correct. Moltke, seeing the writing on the wall, summoned the officers of the Imperial General Staff to a meeting in the Library Hall of the staff headquarters. After a short description of the situation and the grim possibilities for the future, he dismissed them with the admonition 'The Fatherland knows that it can always rely upon the General Staff.' It was the last time Moltke was to meet his staff officers as a group.

It was generally expected that spies of the traditional sort would be at their most useful when the frontiers were closed. On the contrary, during the moves which preceded and followed the outbreak of war and while conditions were rapidly changing, they were to prove of little use. Nicolai therefore temporarily lost not only more of his sources but much of his importance. However, Moltke suddenly discovered that no arrangements had been made to keep German public opinion informed of the course of the war, and Nicolai was given a role which would today embrace both public relations and Press censorship, and which would keep him busy. Once, when delivering a message to Bethmann-Hollweg, the Imperial Chancellor said to him: 'Do tell me how things are with the enemy. I hear nothing at all about that.'*

Not only had spies lost much of their importance, but with the start of the campaign in the West the whole pattern of German Intelligence organization was undergoing changes. Hitherto Nicolai and his web of secret agents had been the main source of information to Moltke. Now the duty of briefing Moltke was taken over by a Lieutenant-Colonel Hentsch, who when war broke out was appointed head of the Foreign Armies Section (the Intelligence section) of the Imperial General Staff in the field.

Nicolai soon came to the conclusion that, until the fronts had stabilized, he would have little hope of reactivating any kind of effective system of spies and secret agents, capable of supplying the information needed for current operations, and decided that his main usefulness would in future lie in attempts to obtain information about the strength and disposition of Allied reserves beyond the immediate areas of operations, and about the longer-term strategic intentions of the Allied

....

* Bethmann–Hollweg was blamed for many of Germany's disasters: one morning an equestrian statue of Bismark was found bearing a placard with this doggerel on it:

> Lieber Bismark steig hernieder
> Gieb uns Deine Kräfte wieder
> Lass in diesen schweren Zeiten
> Lieber Bethmann-Hollweg reiten.

'Dear Bismark, come down from your pedestal and put your skill once more at our disposal. In these difficult times it would be much better to let Bethmann-Hollweg ride the horse.'

leaders. In this he was largely unsuccessful, as have been almost all secret services through the centuries when faced with such difficult questions.

Nor did he neglect the longer-term prospects. The New World had to be penetrated; as it was almost impossible to infiltrate Germans into America, it became necessary to build up an organization based on Germans and German sympathizers. But their reliability could never be properly assessed. In fact, it was not until the United States entered the war and American troops began to disembark at French ports that Nicolai was able to obtain any useful information about their strength and capabilities. He also had to deal with an outbreak of spy fever which, as in Britain and France, swept Germany in the early days of the war. Motor cars packed with gold were said to be crossing into Germany to pay the agents who were everywhere searching out the secrets of the Fatherland. As a result, many distinguished and innocent persons were arrested and subjected to severe interrogation.

During the whole course of the war Nicolai continued, somewhat reluctantly, to hold his post as head of the German secret service, but his activities were severely curtailed and he was no longer permitted to pass his secret reports direct to commanders. They had first to be evaluated by the Foreign Armies Section. Time after time he asked to be relieved of his appointment and sent to a command at the front, but he was refused. In October 1918 when Ludendorff resigned from his post as Hindenberg's Chief of Staff, Nicolai also offered his resignation but General Groener, Ludendorff's successor, refused to consider it because of the importance of the Intelligence function during the armistice and peace negotiations that were obviously about to take place. After the end of the war, Nicolai was much blamed for the failure of his Service to provide reliable and accurate information about the state of Allied reserves, and particularly about the arrival of American forces in Europe. Because of these attacks, and because the maintenance of a secret service was impossible once the revolution had taken hold in Germany, the Supreme Command decided that he was expendable. He tried to obtain an appointment with the Frontier Defence Corps, but was refused on political grounds, and sent on indefinite leave. He reached no rank higher than Colonel, and retired to live in Berlin, feeling himself ill-rewarded for his services to his countrymen. In his later years he became pathologically afraid of the spies whom he believed were threatening the Fatherland, and particularly those of the French Secret Service. He published two books. The first, in 1920, was an uninteresting study of the Press and the effect of Press reports on morale. The second entitled, *The German Secret Service* (1923), was withdrawn from circulation when its author was declared a traitor by the Nazis.

Of Nicolai's ultimate fate little is known. We can only suppose that he became a victim of the Nazi regime. His story, however, is not without significance. As head of a secret service and a director and manipulator of spies, he created for himself a powerful position in the councils of the top echelons of Germany. He reported direct to Moltke and there is little evidence that his information was either checked, evaluated or compared with material from other sources. During the critical period in July 1914 there was little contact between the German political and military authorities on Intelligence matters, and information which might affect vital political decisions—such as the report from one of Nicolai's officers that Russian mobilization was complete—was accepted without question, or on the personal word of the officer concerned. Like so many nations before and since Germany had no system whereby the Intelligence obtained from spies could be checked and placed in a proper perspective, and no co-ordinated system whereby military, political and economic information could be brought together and evaluated as a whole.

★

The German hopes of a rapid and crushing victory in the West in 1914 depended on the so-called Schlieffen Plan, which had been devised by Count Schlieffen, the Chief of the General Staff in the 1890s, whose birthday was annually celebrated by the General Staff with solemn ceremony. His plan, which was developed in the early 1900s and handed in 1906 to Moltke, his successor, was in the event of a two-front war to concentrate the great bulk of German forces in the West and deliver a decisive blow against France to eliminate her from the war before the slow moving Russians could complete their mobilization and take any effective action in the East. For success, therefore, the operation depended on exact knowledge of the Allies' mobilization arrangements and the timings of their various moves. These Nicolai was able to provide. In detail the plan divided the German front in the West into two. The south was to be allotted a minimum number of first-line troops and remain on the defensive. The northern half—which included the bulk of the German Army—would carry out a gigantic wheeling movement, crossing Belgium and debouching into France. The outer edge of the wheel would move southwards to Paris. As the advance proceeded troops from the southern front would be fed into the northern offensive, and the French Army and any Belgian and British troops who had joined the battle would be destroyed by it.

Schlieffen believed that the operation could be completed and France beaten in six weeks. The Russians could be held at bay for this period with as few as ten German divisions, assisted by their Austro-Hungarian allies. In fact, however, the capabilities of the Dual Monarchy were likely to be limited. Colonel Alfred Redl, the former Chief of the Austro-Hungarian Intelligence Department, had been in the pay of Russia for some ten years until his unmasking in 1913. In the course of the eventual investigation into his activities, it emerged that there was very little of military importance that he had not passed to his Russian masters. The Russians were in possession of the documents which contained full details of the campaign by means of which the Austro-Hungarian Government intended to attack and annex Serbia. As a spy Redl was exceptional, but in addition he was perfectly positioned to be a fine 'agent of influence', and in his role as head of Intelligence he was able to prevent the Dual Monarchy from arriving at even a reasonable appreciation of Russian strength and Russian plans. Few have matched Redl's performance, but his individual story, like that of many other spies of greater or lesser ability, was tragic. He was a homosexual who needed money in order to enjoy a high standard of living and gratify his personal desires, and on whose acquisitive instincts the Russian spy-masters were able to play. On being confronted with evidence obtained from postal censorship in Vienna, he confessed and in effect asked to be permitted to shoot himself. This he did in the Hotel Klomser in May 1913; and the full story was immediately and naturally hushed up by the Austro-Hungarian authorities.

There was a good deal to be said in favour of the original simplicity of the Schlieffen Plan, but by 1914 changes had been made to it. Moltke was less ruthless, or perhaps less bold and optimistic, than his predecessor, and he also came under pressure from the ambitious commanders of his armies on the southern flank. In one way or another he ended by reducing the balance of forces between the north and south fronts from the eight to one envisaged in the Schlieffen Plan to an eventual three to one.

On 16 August a million men in seven armies were ranged from north to south along the frontiers of Belgium and France. Of the two key armies, the First in the north was commanded by General von Kluck, a ruthless and ambitious man who at the age of sixty-eight still had an energetic grasp of affairs. In the initial stages he was under the temporary orders of Commander, Second Army, General von Bülow. This turned out to be an unfortunate arrangement, for Kluck had no great opinion of Bülow, thinking him slow, over-cautious and pessimistic—a commander who had acquired a great peacetime reputation for his military ability, but had no experience of command in the field.*

Moltke and his staff, including Lieutenant-Colonel Hentsch, Chief of the Foreign Armies Section, were far behind the armies, at Supreme Headquarters in Coblenz. He had travelled from Berlin in a special train, just as his successors were to do twenty-six years later. With him were the Kaiser and his military, naval and civil cabinets. There were generals and admirals and high-ranking civil servants, each with his own suite or staff of advisers and counsellors. There were chamberlains and their deputies, equerries, secretaries of state and diplomats, order-lies and servants, all in such numbers that the staffs could be accommodated at the standards they required in nothing less than a large city. It would have been helpful to Moltke if his headquarters had been physically separated from the Kaiser, who had unwisely been led to believe that he was gifted in military affairs, but such an arrangement was not possible. In 1914 radio was in its infancy—the German Supreme Head-quarters possessed only one set—and transmissions usually took more than twelve hours to reach their destination, even when the equipment managed to function; often a message had to be repeated many times before its approximate gist became clear. Telephone and telegraph communications were scarcely available, and there were very few

---

* Farther south were the Third Army under Baron von Hausen, another sick man, the Fourth Army under Duke Albrecht of Wurttemberg, the Fifth Army in the Metz–Thionville area under the Imperial Crown Prince, the Sixth Army commanded by Crown Prince Rupprecht and finally the Seventh Army between Strasbourg and the Swiss frontier under General von Heeringen, an ex-Minister of War.

means by which determined commanders in the field could be controlled, even if it were clear to Supreme Headquarters what was happening at the front.

Operations commenced early in August. The German Supreme Command could claim overwhelming success in Belgium and northern France, although tangible proofs were few and some sceptical voices were raised. Kluck, for example, pointedly informed Moltke that, although repeated victories were being claimed by the Germans, nevertheless all the army commanders except himself were crying for help. In fact, time was running out for the Germans. The key to the Schlieffen Plan had been the rapidity of the advance, and it was now beginning to slow. There were many reasons for this. The British Expeditionary Force was in position sooner than expected; the Belgians had escaped the German net and had been able to fall back on the forts of Antwerp; troops had been diverted to the Russian front. Nevertheless, the vast encircling movement continued, but lines of communication were continuously lengthening, and the German forces available to carry on the advance were gradually weakening. Reports were beginning to come in that French troops were being transferred from the southern front to the Paris area, where they could obviously present a threat to the flanks of the advancing German armies.

Supreme Headquarters with all their impedimenta had by now moved to Luxembourg and unease was in the air there. Moltke was gradually becoming aware that his commanders in the field knew little of what was happening; in particular, it was quite clear that Kluck was ignorant of events on any front except his own and not much better informed of the situation there. What was not so clear to Moltke was that he himself was, if possible, even less informed. His armies were marching in blissful ignorance into a giant salient between Paris and Verdun, their logistic problems increasing with every step, and with French troops gathering on Kluck's right flank. His first duty must be to protect the flanks, and orders were issued on 4 September that the First and Second Armies should halt what was to have been the decisive advance and turn to face Paris. To those in the field these orders were incomprehensible. To take up the positions suggested by Moltke would mean that Kluck must retrace his steps and give up much that he had won.

It was at this point that Moltke decided to send Hentsch to First Army to explain the reasons for the orders issued by the Supreme Command. Hentsch would on return be able to inform Moltke of the situation in the field, and thus perhaps resolve some of the latter's growing doubts about the general situation.

Hentsch was a Saxon, who both temperamentally and physically had a good deal in common with Moltke, for he was despondent by nature and suffered from a chronic disease of the gall bladder. In 1914 he was still young for his rank and in appearance somewhat different from the typical German officer. He had a rather fine face, with a sensitive mouth and gentle eyes, and descriptions of his activities show that he had little of the arrogance associated with a graduate of the General Staff. There is no evidence that he had any outstanding intellectual ability; he was, however, adept at summing up a situation, and a certain charm and ease of manner made him a convincing exponent of any idea. His brother officers regarded him as an honest man, in whom they could have confidence; he himself found relations with others somewhat difficult and as a result was not always aware of the cross-currents of information and gossip in the headquarters at which he served.

On 5 September Hentsch set off with one companion on his journey to the right wing. He found Kluck's headquarters to be much farther south than he had expected, but learnt that Kluck, in spite of his irritation with Supreme Headquarters, had already taken some steps to provide protection for the flank of his army. Hentsch outlined the situation as seen from Supreme Headquarters. On the southern front heavy casualties had been suffered and there were few gains to show for them. The evidence was now firm that the French had succeeded in assembling large forces in the Paris area. This was news to Kluck; he had pictured a disorganized enemy in flight and on the point of collapse, being chased to its doom chiefly by his own First Army, perhaps assisted by Bülow and his forces. Behind him he had imagined an over-anxious Supreme Commander, out of touch with the situation, and insisting on unnecessary caution.

The discussion turned to the urgency of the situation. Hentsch did not think there was any requirement for great speed. A French offensive from Paris was not imminent and the German movements could be carried out unhurriedly. This was contrary to the general intention and urgency of Moltke's orders, but Hentsch raised no objection.

What neither he nor Kluck knew was that time was not on their side and that French and British troops were moving into position for a major counterattack, to commence the next morning, 6 September. Kluck complained bitterly that there had been no sign that any such offensive was forthcoming, no disclosures by prisoners, no Intelligence reports, no warning at all.

He decided, however, that further reinforcement of his right flank was required, and the troops he chose for this role were the corps which provided contact with Bülow's army on his left. The effect of this decision was to open a gap between the two armies just opposite the British. When this was pointed out Kluck's arrogant comment was that he had no fear of the British; they had been beaten on several occasions and it would not be easy to persuade them to attack. Even if they did make a move, a cavalry screen and some infantry were available to close the gap. The gap would be twenty-five miles wide; no mean space to be covered by cavalry with exhausted horses.

Hentsch left Kluck and returned to Supreme Headquarters on the evening of 6 September. He gave Moltke a first-hand account of what he had said and done during his visit to the First Army. He pointed to the gap that was emerging between the First and Second Armies as a result of Kluck's decisions. Moltke could do little; he had no reserves immediately at his disposal. In any case the Russians were providing enough problems to keep him fully occupied. He thought it better to let these prima donna generals extricate themselves from the mess they had got themselves into. The German troops might be temporarily halted, they might even suffer reverses, but they would soon recover their poise. One more decisive action, one more heave, and the campaign would be over. Even if he had the resources, he argued, why should he interfere with the presumably competent men in the field?

Bülow, still nominally in command of Kluck, did not view the situation with such confidence. He reported bluntly that it was necessary to plan for a possible enemy breakthrough between his army and Kluck's. Only twenty-four hours had elapsed since Hentsch's return, but the reports reaching Supreme Headquarters were so conflicting that once again Moltke decided he must send someone to make on the spot inquiries, and once again his choice fell on Hentsch. There were many other staff officers at Supreme Headquarters who were capable of carrying out such a mission; in fact, as Hentsch complained somewhat bitterly, the assignment should logically have fallen to an officer of the operations branch. Hentsch had little relish for the second adventure and expressed himself in no uncertain terms about the weight of responsibility which was about to rest on his shoulders. He had a long private discussion with Moltke before he left Supreme Head-quarters. No record of what was said at this meeting appears to exist, and there has been considerable dispute about the exact instructions which Hentsch received. On the one hand it has been suggested (largely by Lieutenant-Colonel von Tappen, Moltke's Chief of Operations) that Hentsch had no authority to authorize any retreats on the part of the armies and was merely on a fact-finding mission. Hentsch himself maintained that he had full powers to act on his own initiative, and that if rearward movements were already in progress he was so to direct them that the gap would be closed. In fact, it seems likely that Hentsch's instructions were ambiguous—in view of Moltke's mental and physical condition and the state of confusion existing at Supreme Headquarters it would have been surprising if they were not. But Hentsch was specifically authorized to give binding instructions in the name of the Supreme Command.

Hentsch left Supreme Headquarters with two companions on the morning of 8 September. This time, and most surprisingly in view of the urgency of the situation, he took a more roundabout route to the Marne front. He first paid visits to the Fifth, Fourth and Third Armies and only afterwards moved north to Bülow and Kluck. His first three visits were satisfactory; he found that the troops were in good heart and fighting vigorously and there was a general air of optimism at the various headquarters. He telephoned to Moltke to say that all was well and reported favourably on the situation.

It was late in the evening of the same day when he arrived at the Château de Montmort, the headquarters of the Second Army. Bülow had just returned from a visit to the front. He was tired and worried. The right wing of his army had already had to start pulling back because of strong enemy pressure. Everyone knew from peacetime manœuvres that Bülow believed in 'shoulder to shoulder' tactics and his operational orders invariably allotted boundaries to even quite small units. Not for him were open flanks. At the age of sixty-eight one does not run many risks and he regarded it as essential that the First and

Third Armies on either side of him kept close and left no gaps between them. In his view the situation could only be retrieved by a co-ordinated withdrawal of the armies. The meeting went on until midnight when discussion came to a desultory conclusion. Although Hentsch was thoroughly disillusioned by the apparent lack of spirit on the part of the German troops and their leaders he reported to Moltke that while the situation of the Second Army was serious it was not hopeless.

Hentsch was up early next morning for a meeting at 5.30 a.m. The overnight reports did not add much that was new. Tempers were still somewhat frayed, but Hentsch seems to have made up his mind that the only solution was for the two northern armies to withdraw on converging lines and thus once more create a continuous front, and when Bülow finally announced his intention of giving orders for the withdrawal of the Second Army across the Marne, Hentsch signified his approval and left.

He had now some sixty miles to cover to reach the First Army Headquarters at Mareuil. His car ran into endless obstructions and he took seven hours to do the journey. Convoys of wounded mingled with units already in retreat and blocked the road; from time to time Hentsch himself had to dismount and clear a way. It was not until well after noon that he reached his destination. For some reason he did not see von Kluck himself (who complained about this neglect), but explained the situation regarding the Second Army to his Chief of Staff, a General von Kuhl to whom Hentsch was well known as he had previously served under him. The confusion Hentsch had witnessed on his journey had served to increase his pessimism and he reminded Kuhl that since the whole of Bülow's army would soon be withdrawing, the First Army would clearly have to conform, and he sketched the lines to be reached by the armies on the Chief of Staff's map with charcoal. General von Kuhl maintained that the situation of the First Army was by no means hopeless, although he admitted that there had already been some withdrawal on the left when it was supporting Bülow. Otherwise their forces were now in a position to counter the French threat and at the moment the British were advancing slowly and presenting no obvious problems. By the evening victory could lie with the Germans, and Hentsch and Bülow would no longer need to take counsel of their fears.

Much as Hentsch might have liked to accept these reassurances, he could not bring himself to believe from what he had seen and heard that a local success by Kluck's troops could possibly retrieve the general situation. The Second Army was already on the move to the rear and confusion was spreading. He insisted, as Moltke's representative, that the First Army must withdraw in a north-easterly direction. Kuhl, perhaps against his better judgement, was persuaded by Hentsch's arguments, and departed to find his master, General von Kluck. In view of what we know of the latter's irascible character, it is easy to understand the outburst with which he greeted Hentsch's proposals. Nevertheless, perhaps partly because of his respect for a member of the General Staff and an emissary of Moltke, he issued the order to withdraw. In effect, this order conceded to the Allies victory in the battle of the Marne, and in a sense ensured eventual German defeat in World War I.

Hentsch, having delivered his bombshell at First Army, started back to Luxembourg, following his same route, but in a reverse direction. When he reached the southern front he was faced with a new problem. A withdrawal by the northerly armies on the scale that had been agreed would expose the flank of the Third Army, and a retreat here would expose the flank of the Fourth Army, and so on. Hausen and Duke Albrecht made no difficulties, but the Imperial Crown Prince at Fifth Army had been enjoying some successes near Verdun, and was in no mood to break off his action and conduct an immediate retreat. He bluntly asked Hentsch for his written authority to make such suggestions on behalf of Moltke; Hentsch of course had no such credentials and departed on the weary trek back to Supreme Headquarters with this ticklish problem unsettled.

Moltke, in the meantime, had explained the situation to the Kaiser, who was shaken by the news, complaining that until this moment he had heard of nothing but victories, but he was better off than the German public who heard nothing of the disasters until 23 September. Moltke had always thoroughly disliked briefing his Royal master, for whom he had no professional regard, but this was the most difficult interrogation he had faced. He himself had no doubt of the correctness of the decision to withdraw, although his own Chief of Operations and many other officers at the headquarters opposed it.

However, Hentsch's personal report, on his return to Supreme Headquarters, cheered Moltke a little. The withdrawal would present no great difficulty as enemy pursuit was slow. Perhaps a limited retreat, followed by a consolidation and regrouping, did not mean disaster. The time might not be far off when the German armies could resume the offensive; this might be possible in as little as two or three days. Opportunities for self-deception were vast, especially as Hentsch had a plan that demanded action. His chief recommendation was that Moltke himself should immediately visit the front, see the situation at first hand, confirm the measures already taken, tackle the problem posed by the refusal of the armies in the south to withdraw, and consider future plans and operations.

Early in the morning of 11 September Moltke and his convoy set out for the front. The Imperial Crown Prince at Fifth Army had to be given a formal command to cease offensive operations, and did not relish taking orders from one whom he later described as a broken man making superhuman efforts to hold back his tears. At Third Army the commander, General Hausen, was ill in bed and all was confusion and despondency. At Bülow's Second Army Headquarters the discussion was long and acrimonious, but the plans for withdrawal were not altered, and there was no talk of further offensives. Moltke did not visit First Army, but even the optimistic Kluck had by now changed his views. His army was exhausted and confused, and the morale of all the German forces was under strain. He had had to reverse the order of march of many thousands of men with their artillery, transport and baggage; what was even more difficult, he had to explain these actions to the officers and men of an army which considered victory to be nearly within its grasp. All was well while victory was in sight; retreat was another matter.

Moltke returned to his headquarters, exhausted. Gradually the conviction grew amongst his staff that he was incapable of directing further operations and must be replaced. The problem was put before the Kaiser, whose main concern was that a change of command should not be interpreted as an acknowledgement of a German defeat. He suggested that Moltke's health made a long rest imperative. The final compromise was simple. Moltke's name would continue to appear on all orders and instructions, but he would forthwith be relieved of all duties. General Erich von Falkenhayn, the War Minister, took over on 14 September. And with the change in command came a change in strategy. Gone were the plans for a sweeping war of movement, gone was the impetus towards rapid and annihilating victory; instead the German Supreme Command settled down to a long and static war of attrition.

At least indirectly, their errors in the first two weeks of September 1914 cost the Germans the war, and a great deal has been written about the blame that should be allocated to the officers concerned, from Moltke through Hentsch to Bülow, Kluck and Kuhl. Interest naturally centres on Hentsch, the man of Intelligence prised from his desk at Supreme Headquarters to become the emissary of the Chief of Staff of the Imperial Armies.

Rumours circulated in Germany that the débâcle had been due to a Saxon staff officer who had given a wrong order to Prussian troops to retire. His name was Hentsch and he had been court-martialled and shot for his misjudgement.

Hentsch consistently maintained that he had never exceeded his instructions and that he could not be held responsible for the operational decisions of von Bülow who, taking counsel of his fears, had decided to withdraw. Bülow had at one time been looked upon as the natural successor to von Schlieffen and the Kaiser had a high opinion of his military judgement: who was Hentsch to dispute this? It was not until a year after Hentsch's death in Rumania, where he became Chief of Staff to an army, that Ludendorff ordered an inquiry into the whole circumstances of the affair. But the Imperial General Staff could not be induced to repudiate one of its members, and Hentsch's actions were considered to be justified in that he did not go beyond what he was entitled to do. Whether a retreat was in fact necessary was left to historians of the future to decide.

It is, however, not the purpose of this narrative to discuss this problem in detail but to discuss its Intelligence relevance. The battle had not yet been fought and its outcome could still depend upon the nerves and wills of the opposing commanders.

Whatever the ultimate allocation of responsibility amongst the German officers concerned, Hentsch, both because of his temperament and because of his training and his experiences as an Intelligence officer, was the wrong man for the role he had to play. By temperament he was pessimistic, a quality which he, unfortunately for the Germans, shared with Moltke and Bülow. As an Intelligence officer he undoubtedly suffered from the tendency which all Intelligence officers possess to a greater or lesser degree—the tendency to overrate the relative strength and capabilities of their opponents. The Allies were experiencing major difficulties. Joffre for example had been compelled to rid himself of more than one hundred and thirty generals and senior officers in the past few weeks on grounds of sheer incompetence. Relations between the British and French commands had not been without friction and at one moment the British General French had wanted to withdraw his troops from the battle altogether for rest and refitting until he was persuaded otherwise. In addition there were logistic problems facing the Allies in spite of their short and interior lines of supply, and the French artillery which at the beginning of the war had surprised the Germans by its accuracy and mobility, was already running out of ammunition.

Intelligence officers are quite aware that they lack a good deal of information about the enemy; because they know so much, they are often particularly over-conscious of what they do not know. Often they feel compelled to compensate for this lack of complete information by minimizing the enemy's difficulties and the constraints under which he must operate, and overrating the problems facing friendly forces. In short, an Intelligence officer is probably the least suitable person to make what has come to be known as a 'net' estimate of a situation—an estimate which takes into account the relative capabilities and probable intentions of both sides in a struggle, and attempts to arrive at a reasoned and balanced judgement; the advice of an Intelligence officer will almost always tend to err on the side of prudence. During the critical September days prudential advice was the last thing the German Command required, and the translation of this prudential advice into orders in the field was disastrous.

There has perhaps been too great a willingness to blame Hentsch for the débâcle. In his position, and with his background, it was probably impossible for him to act differently. Moltke was the true architect of defeat. First, he chose Hentsch for the mission; he chose a member of the General Staff in whom he had confidence, and sophisticated considerations concerning the psychological tendencies of Intelligence officers were almost certainly far from his mind at the time he was making the choice. Secondly, he was divorced from events at the front and for this he can fairly be blamed, although there were a number of mitigating circumstances. He was also a sick man, and his illnesses undoubtedly affected his judgement. His tragic outburst to General von Einem, 'Heavens above, how could this have happened to me?', was a sign of his despairing spirit.

Moltke was also locked into an inflexible command structure and outdated procedures. A theory had grown up in the German Army that the vast numbers of men engaged in modern war and the scope of modern operations would not permit any effective and continuing centralized command. During the big battles of the Franco-Prussian war of 1870 the Chief of the General Staff had remained with his Sovereign and the military machine had been allowed to take its pre-planned course. Once battle was joined, the theory ran, it was too late to introduce new elements into the problem; no new Intelligence, no new appreciations could be permitted to alter the plans carefully prepared in peacetime. This was the structure and the system which Moltke inherited and when the unexpected happened he was unequal to the task of exerting strong and direct control. He found himself unable to break from the Kaiser and traditional procedures and to move forward with a small staff to the battle areas.

Finally, he lacked Intelligence. The Secret Service, as we have seen, failed to keep up with the sweeping advances of the opening days of the war. The main sources of tactical information about enemy forces were the forward German troops in contact with them, but the organization which existed at the various levels of command to obtain information from interrogations and captured documents, sift and analyse it and forward the results rapidly to Supreme Headquarters was faulty and in some areas non-existent. As the front became more confused and the fog of battle descended, Moltke was at a loss, and could do no more than send someone he trusted to investigate and give orders on his behalf.

What is difficult to understand is how a general who was reckoned to be one of the finest products of the German military system could be so inept. In World War II General Eisenhower was much criticized, chiefly for his lack of experience in high command, but he made few mistakes compared with the allegedly experienced Moltke. It is true of course that Moltke was sixty-six in 1914, while Eisenhower was in his early fifties in the latter stages of World War II. Moltke was a sick man, while Eisenhower enjoyed excellent health; he could relax when opportunities arose and found his greatest pleasure in the company of those he commanded, whether they were personal friends like Bradley, or ordinary soldiers. Nevertheless Eisenhower demonstrated a technique of military command that was vastly superior to that shown by Moltke. His headquarters was happy and the staff divisions co-operative. Although he listened to the arguments of his subordinate commanders such as Montgomery and Bradley, it was he who finally called them to order and made (and enforced) the ultimate decisions. Far from sitting at a headquarters many miles from the front, Eisenhower paid constant visits to his commanders and was in close touch with the troops. It was, however, particularly in his relations with his superiors that Eisenhower showed his mastery. Moltke's narrow and entirely professional training did not fit him to face the Kaiser and the German War Cabinet with anything approaching poise or equanimity. Eisenhower's actual military experience was infinitely less than that of Moltke, but he possessed a reserve of experience of other than military affairs which enabled him to stand his ground when faced with Prime Ministers or Presidents and refuse to accept their interference with his decisions. Possibly the fact that Eisenhower came from a young and virile nation, whereas Moltke was a representative of an age that was passing, had a good deal to do with the matter.

The continuing naïveté of German officers in other than strictly military matters was demonstrated in the late 1930s by the cases of Field-Marshal von Blomberg, the German War Minister, and General von Fritsch, the Commander-in-Chief of the Army, two of the most outstanding officers of the period. Blomberg, who had been chosen to lead Germany's forces when the Nazi regime came to power and who became the first field-marshal of the Third Reich, had been a widower for some years in 1937. He was a gentle and idealistic man, and of such simplicity and unworldliness that he managed to marry, apparently in all innocence, a masseuse who was discovered to have a police record as a prostitute. What is more, he invited Hitler and Goering to be witnesses at the wedding, and later rejected all suggestions that he should divorce the lady. There were in fact strong political reasons why Hitler wished to remove Blomberg from his position, but this unfortunate marriage with a woman of inferior standing and the social solecism he committed in inviting the Führer to be a witness were made the excuses. Hitler announced the dismissal at a meeting of senior officers of the armed forces in the Reichs Chancellery in Berlin on the afternoon of 14 February 1938; he said that Blomberg's activities had been a great disappointment to him and added that he personally would now assume the role of guardian of the honour of the officers of the German Army. The assembled officers could only acquiesce, almost all of them convinced that the slur cast by Blomberg upon the officer class fully justified his dismissal.

General von Fritsch was dismissed at the same time, but his case was rather different. He was a strong opponent of Hitler, and the charge against him was homosexuality. He was later fully cleared by a court of inquiry, and the charge was proved to have been trumped up by the Gestapo with the object of discrediting the Army. Fritsch, however, received no word of regret or apology from the Führer for the way in which he had been treated; as long as he lived he sighed for the loss of his military career. His views were naïve in the extreme. He firmly believed that Germany was fighting three justified battles, one against International Jewry, one against the working classes, and the third against the ultramontane faith of the Roman Catholic Church. He faced the fact that these were in effect wars with Great Britain and the United States, and he realized that an agreement with the Soviet Union was the only course open to Germany, no matter how repulsive the ruling classes in Russia might be. To my mind, the stupidity of Blomberg in his matrimonial affairs, and the naïveté of Fritsch in international matters throw into stark relief the deficiences of the meticulous German military training, and the unreality of the German tradition that an officer should confine himself strictly to military affairs at the expense of gaining a wider knowledge of the world.

It is extraordinarily difficult to judge how to choose men for high command, and how great commanders should be sought out and trained. The high offices they will be called upon to fill have very few counterparts in peacetime affairs, and most nations have created special centres of education for senior officers, where they can be brought into contact with senior civil servants and other civilians. Politicians, officials and magnates from industry lecture these students; military history is studied somewhat perfunctorily; and visits to other countries to study campaigns and peoples are arranged. Undoubtedly this form of education has a great deal of merit, but I believe that a good deal more is required of those who aspire to the highest command levels. Such men have got to learn something that it is almost impossible to teach—how to handle men, both masters and subordinates. In times of crisis, a supreme commander must either, like Moltke, leave his subordinates to their own devices and explain situations apologetically to his superiors, or, like Eisenhower, listen patiently to the arguments of subordinates and then crack the whip, and firmly defend his decisions before his own masters.

*

Unlike Nicolai and Hentsch, John Charteris, a British officer, came somewhat reluctantly to the field of Intelligence, without training or experience. He was a young engineer officer who had served on the staff of Sir Douglas Haig in India. Haig was always loyal to the officers who had served with him there, and when he was given command of one of the two British corps on the outbreak of World War I he chose Charteris as the head of his corps Intelligence section. Three months later at the end of December 1914 when Haig was appointed to command the British First Army Charteris became a lieutenant-colonel and the head of Intelligence at the army headquarters. In December 1915 Field-Marshal Sir John French, the Commander-in-Chief of the British Expeditionary Force, was deemed to have lost the confidence of the British Government and was replaced by Haig. Charteris in due course became a brigadier-general and the head of the Intelligence staff at Haig's General Headquarters. Now, after a meteoric rise, he was the chief Intelligence officer of the largest army Britain had ever sent overseas, with responsibilities including censorship, cyphers, maps, visitors, liaison with foreign governments and press correspondents.

It is perhaps kindest to judge Charteris in light of the general atmosphere which prevailed at British G.H.Q. in those days. At the summit was Sir Douglas Haig, the British Commander-in-Chief. He was a respected if unexciting British General, perhaps a little slow thinking and certainly not articulate. Politicians were his natural enemies and what seemed to annoy him most about them was their self-satisfaction. It might not be entirely fair to label him as pig-headed, for he willingly listened to contrary opinions, yet once having made up his mind it seems he seldom changed it. His persistence in continuing attacks such as those at Passchendaele when everything seemed stacked against him sprang less from an under-rating of his opponent than from his study of military history and a deep conviction that the premature abandonment of an enterprise could lead only to moral and psychological disaster. The events of September 1914 and the Hentsch affair had perhaps reinforced this conviction—a little more persistence by the Germans and victory might well have been theirs at the Marne.

There were not many outstanding men close to Haig. General Kiggell, his Chief of Staff, was already worn out. In a generally affluent peacetime corps of officers he had struggled to the top, handicapped by a lack of private resources; when war came he was already in need of a long rest. Neither he nor the Chief of Operations, General Davidson, an industrious but not very clever staff officer, were really in touch with conditions at the front. They relied on reports of liaison officers to keep them informed, but liaison officers cannot always put down on paper the sort of things a commander should know. Moreover, the exaggerated secrecy of the operations branch regarding its plans and intentions did not make work at G.H.Q. any easier, or promote a happy and trusting atmosphere among the staff.

It was with these men that Charteris had to work and it was these men and others like them who passed the final and unfavourable judgement on his activities. Haig, in contrast to his predecessor, Sir John French, who paid small heed to the estimates put before him, had right from the beginning realized the requirement for an effective Intelligence organization. Undoubtedly much of his interest was due to his previous study of foreign armies. In 1893 and again a year later he had been a close observer of the French Army manœvures and had also been able to watch the German Army at work. In common with many of the British officers who participated in such visits he returned home with gloomy fears about the future and with a new understanding of the German anxiety and ability to conceal its military secrets, and thus of the need for an Intelligence effort to find out what they were really up to and how efficient they were. Haig kept in the closest touch with Charteris. He saw him frequently and ensured that Charteris attended all important meetings where his advice and information could be of value. Socially, Charteris was invariably at the centre of things. Right from 14 August when Haig had attended a picnic Champagne lunch before embarking for France and Charteris was present, few dinners or luncheon parties at G.H.Q. were complete without his presence; in fact at times he presided at these functions in place of Haig. And no distinguished guest escaped his net, whether it was the French Prime

Minister who asked leave to show his Intelligence estimates to the French Cabinet, or Lloyd George, the British Prime Minister, who disliked Charteris even more than he disliked his master.

Haig did, however, impose stringent and rather curious demands upon his Intelligence staff. He required, for example, that every estimate or Intelligence document he received should be clearly and formally divided into 'fact', 'probability', 'possibility' and 'improbability'. Charteris was by nature an optimist, and his optimism was described by one of his junior officers as acting like a tonic on the morale of his commander. Unfortunately, he sometimes tended to allow his optimism to override his wisdom. Having a better brain than most of his contemporaries, he was not universally popular in the Army either with his equals or subordinates. On the other hand, he knew his job thoroughly, and Haig knew this. Charteris believed that Intelligence duties demanded a good deal of healthy scepticism, and he followed the simple and sound rule that no information should be accepted as probable unless it was confirmed by at least two independent sources; when he reported that something or other seemed 'not improbable', he usually meant that it was practically certain.

Charteris sometimes went to considerable lengths to provide Haig with attractive details and to conceal unappealing items. The story is told, for example, that on one occasion after the Battle of the Somme, when the British had few successes to report, Charteris took Haig to visit a camp for German prisoners of war. In order to give Haig the impression that the German Army was largely composed of men of poor physique, Charteris had all the able-bodied and unwounded prisoners removed from the camp before the visit. On another occasion, he made similar arrangements for a visit to the front by Lloyd George.

To the purist this may seem a considerable crime but it should be remembered that a commander tends to hear a great deal of depressing information. If an Intelligence officer can with a clear conscience report favourable items, these can help to lighten the heavy load a commander bears. This point was brought home to me when I was with Eisenhower in North Africa in World War II. I was able to assure him that in spite of the near-disaster at Kasserine the American troops, faced by overwhelming odds and experienced enemy commanders, had acquitted themselves with distinction, and the atmosphere at the headquarters lightened considerably. I do not excuse Charteris if he had less regard for the truth than was appropriate in the circumstances, but I can at least appreciate his dilemmas.

During 1916 and 1917 there was no lack of Intelligence about the German armies on the Western Front. The main sources of information were the interrogation of prisoners of war and the examination of captured documents, although air photography was being developed rapidly. There were few reports of value from spies or secret agents, but attempts were occasionally made to use rather more novel systems. At one point carrier pigeons were dropped by parachute in German-occupied territory, with questionnaires in capsules attached to their legs. The hope was that whoever found a pigeon would quickly answer the questions, replace the questionnaire in the container, and point the bird towards the West. I have no idea how many questionnaires were actually returned by this method, but it is known that many people were summarily executed by the Germans for completing them.

In spite of the availability of information Charteris does not seem to have gained any real insight into the changes which the German Army was undergoing during this period, and he appears even less aware of conditions on the German Home Front. He had little confidence in French Intelligence, asserting that French estimates were valueless and that French Intelligence staffs decided what they would like to happen and then manufactured evidence to demonstrate that it was in fact happening. He therefore depended to a large extent on the general information provided by the War Office in London. Although information from this source was excellent Haig seems too often to have been presented only with scraps of uncollated items which gave him a distorted picture of the real situation, both in strategic and tactical terms. He wrote in his diary, for example, that extracts from recently captured German correspondence were most encouraging; hunger, sickness, riots and disorder were spreading rapidly throughout the Fatherland. This was not true. The Home Front in Germany at the time was in reasonable order, while the disintegration of the Russian forces in the East, under the influence of Bolshevism and the coming revolution, was having the effect of freeing more German troops for use in the West.

It appears to have been left to Charteris to advise Haig about the significance of the peace proposals put forward by Germany at the end of 1916, and the Austrian approaches to Russia in April 1917. Charteris apparently found these politico-military problems perplexing, but his optimistic nature caused him to exaggerate their importance. In spite of his inclination to believe that Germany was collapsing, and that one more strong push would end the war, he found himself also puzzled about the state of the enemy's morale, one of the most difficult problems with which Intelligence officers can be faced in operations. The question is one of subjective judgement and the masses of reports on this subject are invariably conflicting. In North Africa and Europe in World War II there were constant reports that German morale was weakening, while our troops in the front line found that German soldiers usually fought with astonishing bravery and determination until they were killed or captured, even in the most hopeless circumstances. The only guide to estimating morale is experience, both in Intelligence and in military matters. In my opinion, the last persons to whom such assessments should be left are experts in political warfare and propaganda, who cannot generally be relied upon for unbiased judgement in this field.

It was in more general and longer-term issues such as these that Charteris's judgements were often particularly poor, and on at least one occasion Haig made over-optimistic statements to the Press as a consequence of his advice.

As a result of this, and other criticism, Charteris was becoming a controversial figure and the subject of adverse comment by members of the War Cabinet in London, who began to see in him Haig's *eminence grise*. Within the Army Charteris was being criticized also. His youth—he had become known in senior military circles as the 'Principal Boy'—and his rapid promotions were not regarded with a great deal of favour; in principle, and even in wartime, the services were still wedded to seniority as the main element in eligibility for promotion. Further, his colleagues in the field regarded him as usually over-optimistic. Nevertheless, he still had Haig's confidence. He remained close to the Commander-in-Chief and continued to brief him on general political and economic as well as purely tactical matters.

One subject in which Haig took great interest, for example, was the question of German manpower reserves. It is surprising to read that he reported in the summer of 1917 that if fighting continued at its then current intensity for six months Germany would have come to the end of her available manpower. It should surely have been obvious to Charteris and Haig that such judgements of manpower situations are similar to economic appreciations—the imponderables are so great that sensible estimates are complex. Certainly dogmatic statements about reaching the end of manpower pools have little meaning, because manpower resources can be enlarged in so many ways, by lowering the minimum age for military service, by combing out industry, by using female labour, by shortening periods of convalescence for the sick and wounded and so on. No one can foresee with any certitude which, or which combination, of these expedients an enemy is likely to adopt, and thus estimates of the resulting situations can only be equivocal. Similar arguments can be applied to most forms of relatively unsophisticated forecasting related to economic warfare. Belts can always be drawn tighter, and economic sanctions are unlikely to be effective in the absence of very rigorous and strict controls.

The major and final controversy surrounding Charteris as an Intelligence officer arose from the Battle of Cambrai in November 1917. This was the first true tank battle of World War I, and resulted from Haig's plan to attack the Germans south of Cambrai in order to relieve growing pressure on the adjacent French armies. During the summer of 1917 it had become quite clear from captured documents that a number of fresh German divisions had arrived from the Russian front to reinforce the sector near Cambrai which the British were about to attack. The evidence of this movement was presented, fully documented, to Charteris by his staff before the battle, but he refused to accept it, directing that the new divisions should not be shown on any map. He argued that if the Commander-in-Chief were told that the Germans had reinforced the area, he would not necessarily believe it but his confidence would be shaken. In the event, after some early British successes, the Cambrai attack was a great disappointment, and the War Cabinet became convinced that Haig had been shockingly misinformed by his chief Intelligence officer. Things had reached a stage where some reorganization of the Intelligence machine was necessary and urgent.

Charteris had already realized that he was under fire from the politicians at home and had offered his resignation at the beginning of November, before the Cambrai battle. Haig refused this offer at the time, but the outcome of the Cambrai battle together with Charteris's

outspoken criticism of the Intelligence staffs of the Supreme War
Council, forced Haig's hand, and he relieved Charteris of his appoint-
ment in December. Haig wrote later that Charteris had made himself
so unpopular with the authorities at the War Office and the War
Committee of the Cabinet that they almost regarded him as another
Dreyfus.

Rather surprisingly, Charteris was transferred to the appointment of
Deputy Inspector-General of Transportation at the same headquarters.
From his staff position he continued to proffer strategic advice to the
Commander-in-Chief, much to the discomfiture of his successor, Sir
Herbert Lawrence, who was one of the most brilliant brains in the
British Army and was later to become a prominent London banker:
Sir Herbert wasn't allowed to stay in Intelligence for long, because the
Treasury refused to make provision for the pay of a major-general. In
1918, Charteris was sent to Baghdad to an appointment which carried
less pay than he had received when he left India in 1911. Haig con-
tinued to believe that his protégé had been shabbily treated.

There are a number of points of interest about the Haig–Charteris
relationship. Charteris seems on first estimates to have been afraid to
present Haig with facts which he judged to be unpalatable. But this was
not really the case. The truth is that Charteris was profoundly convinced that once Haig had made up his mind on a certain course of
action (and Charteris thought that he seldom erred in the judgements
he formed) no amount of subsequent or contradictory Intelligence would
make him change his views: thus to present unpalatable facts was a
waste of time. This was probably one reason for Charteris's reputation
for unmerited optimism. Thus an extraordinary situation developed in
which Charteris had a reasonable appreciation of events on the German
side of the front but was unable or unwilling to convey this picture to
his commander. There was really no excuse for this, at least as far as
tactical matters were concerned. Longer-term appreciations were a
different matter; in this area too much seems to have been expected of
Charteris and his staff. Field Intelligence staffs are not equipped and
manned to make long-term estimates of such general factors as morale,
manpower, industrial capacity and the effects of propaganda. They are
concerned with the battlefield itself, the movements of enemy reserves,
the arrival of reinforcements on their front, the appearance of new
weapons and tactics. Obviously there is a close relationship between

long- and short-term estimates, but the staffs and attitudes required to produce them are quite different in both quantity and quality. Nevertheless, Charteris appears to have been responsible, or to have made himself responsible, for a good deal of this long-term estimating, and it was from his efforts in this field that many of the more significant accusations of over-optimism and misjudgement arose. On the other hand, some of Charteris's optimistic forecasts proved true. He believed that December 1917 would see the last Christmas of the war, and issued a paper correctly estimating German strategy for 1918, naming not only the month, but also three localities at which the major German attacks of that year would come.

The problems were not all due to Charteris. Haig, in spite of his interest in Intelligence, appears to have been relatively untutored in its nuances. His demands for the rigid categorization of data were unreasonable, and Charteris must have found it extraordinarily difficult to make estimates of the kind that Haig demanded. An Intelligence estimate is a delicate document, which demands a certain subtlety of understanding on the part of the recipient as well as the author.

Charteris was quick-witted, observant, humorous and methodical. He could be a convincing conversationalist when he wanted, but an acute observer would note in him certain character weaknesses and indecision. Some men accused him of making up his mind and drawing conclusions about the enemy without even examining the evidence. This would be unfair to him, but it is true to say that he was intellectually arrogant. I met many such Intelligence officers in World War II, and indeed without such people Intelligence staffs would find it impossible to perform their more crucial and imaginative tasks. Nearly all came from distinguished careers in civilian life, and their so-called arrogance often arose from their undoubted intellectual superiority over their regular service colleagues. Sometimes the serving officers envied or even feared them because of their abilities. In spite of appearances, it is possible that Charteris, perhaps in the very different environment of World War II, perhaps with modern techniques and growing experience, would have made a good Intelligence officer. In World War I, however, he was generally believed to have been a failure; nevertheless, he exemplifies many such officers in the British military Intelligence structure during and after that war—officers posted to Intelligence appointments on a random basis or because of acquaintanceship, and expected to carry out very heavy responsibilities without adequate training or experience.

Many facets of the Haig–Charteris relationship remain unexplained, and this is especially true of the circumstances surrounding Charteris's dismissal. Haig himself refused to accept the proposition that Charteris should be the whipping-boy for the charges of undue optimism brought against himself. He strongly denied a widespread belief that in Intelligence matters he was completely dominated by him and claimed that in forming his judgements he did not depend only on Charteris's estimates and comments, but was in close touch with the commanders at the front. Further, since he had known the German forces intimately since the beginning of the war, he could bring his own experience to bear on Intelligence reports. On the other hand, under pressure he did relieve Charteris of his appointment, although he may have rationalized this decision by assuming that a change of employment would be good for Charteris's career. In his papers he wrote, 'Intelligence is rather a special kind of work and has a very small place in the army in peacetime.'

Perhaps some part of the explanation lies in the controversy over Haig himself. To many politicians he was anathema, and if it could be shown that he was over-dependent upon the advice of staff officers with poor judgement his position could be weakened. In a sense, the forced dismissal of a senior staff officer is a strong criticism of the commander concerned, especially if the staff officer in question has been a protégé of the commander for many years. A great deal of the criticism levelled at Charteris probably represented an indirect attack on Haig.

At the start of World War I 'professionalism' played little part in Intelligence. Intelligence officers like Hentsch and Charteris appear to have had little, if any, training for their jobs, and Intelligence staffs were often regarded as unwelcome and unnecessary additions to headquarters. In fact, so confident were the Germans of success in 1914 that units and formations often left their Intelligence officers behind when they went into battle, like baggage 'not wanted on voyage'; Hentsch, the Chief of *all* Intelligence for the West and the East, was sent perambulating round the countryside on liaison tasks. On the other hand, spies like Redl flourished not only in the popular imagination, but also in fact, and secret services had alarming influence in high quarters in most continental countries.

As World War I progressed a number of much-needed changes were made in the Intelligence organizations of both sides. In Germany the luckless Hentsch was replaced by the highly efficient Colonel von Rauch, who carried on his task with distinction and brilliance until the end of the war, thereby earning high commendation from Ludendorff. In Britain the Intelligence Corps grew to maturity, and by 1917 trained members of this Corps were to be found holding Intelligence appointments—although rarely senior ones—at all the principal headquarters. Technical developments, such as direction-finding and flash-spotting, were introduced, and air photography began to show its tremendous potential. Radio interception and analysis had been in limited use at the start of the war, and this source was developed into a large and relatively efficient machine by the Navy as well as by the Army. But for the first two years of the war at least, crucial decisions affecting the lives of millions were often taken on the flimsiest of evidence, or at least on evidence the reliability of which no one could judge. Spies and agents, who had been expected to provide all the essential information, suddenly found that they were little adapted to the new circumstances. Security tightened and the possibility of obtaining critical facts relating to an opponent's strategy, armaments and long-term plans became remote. Little thought had been given to organizing political and economic Intelligence. Vast centres for spying grew up in countries such as Switzerland and Holland which devoted themselves to the minutiae of Intelligence and promoted a thriving trade in non-essentials and international gossip. But it is no exaggeration to suggest that some of the inadequacies seen in the course of World War I, the mistakes of generalship, the poor strategic planning and the many tactical errors, reflected a serious inability to acquire Intelligence or to make effective and professional use of the Intelligence that *was* available.

2

FRANCE

The Boulevard St Germain in Paris is an unprepossessing street, only a short taxi ride from the Hotel Crillon in the Place de la Concorde, where I used to stay during my visits to Paris in 1939 and 1940. I was then a member of the Directorate of Military Intelligence at the War Office, and my destination was a dull stone building in a courtyard set back from the boulevard. There was a gendarme on duty at the entrance to the courtyard, but the checking of visitors at the main door of the building itself was usually perfunctory. Yet this building housed the headquarters of the world-famous Deuxième Bureau, the Intelligence division of the French General Staff. Inside, the stairs and corridors were both poorly lit and highly polished, a combination that made haste unwise. As I picked my careful way through these passages I used to scrutinize the office doors for any indication of the names of those working within. This, I suppose, was mere force of habit, for at that time just before World War II the French and British Intelligence services worked closely together, and there was no reason for the Deuxième Bureau to conceal from me the names of its officers.

The French Intelligence structure comprised two main divisions, the Deuxième Bureau and the Service de Renseignements (the Cinquième Bureau). The latter was the French secret service—the famous espionage organization which constituted one of the sources of information available to the Deuxième Bureau. The great prestige that attached to the Deuxième Bureau—which was after all merely a part of the staff of the French Army—arose from the fact that the German Navy and the German Air Force counted for little in the higher councils of the French Government. The German Army was thought to be the main enemy, and the Deuxième Bureau was the main provider of Intelligence to the government, and thus in effect if not in name the central Intelligence bureau of France. The head of the Deuxième Bureau for the crucial latter part of the inter-war years was a Colonel Gauché, who was appointed to the post in 1935.

Gauché was a pleasant though ponderous officer, in his later fifties at the beginning of World War II, who had an extraordinary affection for a tame parrot. He was of medium height, but thick set, with greying hair cut short. When I met him I was struck by the intelligent twinkle in his eyes, which peered through pince-nez so precariously balanced that it seemed as if a sneeze might dislodge them. He was I think a Norman, and a little reticent, almost taciturn. It took several months for anyone to get on easy terms with him, and even then the relationship tended to remain somewhat formal. Like all Frenchmen he treated food and drink with due respect and appreciation, and thoroughly enjoyed an informal dinner party with colleagues. Apart from this, little was known of his recreations or his private life. I do not know to this day if he was married or had a family.

On closer business acquaintance his sterling qualities became obvious. Originally he had been an infantry officer and his opinions were always practical and pragmatic. One felt that any advice or information he was prepared to give would be good and reliable. He never appeared to be over-influenced by political events or by his superiors. On the other hand, he had an easy manner with his subordinates who clearly appreciated his experience and abilities in the Intelligence field.

Gauché could read English, though no one ever heard him speak it. In his relations with Britain, he was invariably co-operative and helpful. On the fly-leaf of the copy of his book in the library of the Ministry of Defence in London he has written 'Homage de l'auteur en souvenir des rapports confiants avec les officiers britanniques, en particulier les attachés militaires accredités à Paris.' British officers who are so often tempted to criticize our French friends should perhaps bear in mind this genuine tribute from Gauché. Gauché enjoyed the confidence of most French senior officers and was especially close to General Gamelin, the Chief of the National Defence Staff.

My first official visits to the Deuxième Bureau were in 1939, but these were not my first contacts with France and the French Army. Like many of my generation I was taught French at school, and two of my sisters were sent to complete their education in France. My father, incidentally, decided at the age of sixty-seven that it was imperative for him also to learn French; this caused some confusion and much embarrassment, particularly on the golf course when he insisted that the proceedings should be conducted in French. Somehow, 'Gare devant!' seemed to have less impact on other golfers than 'Fore!'

It was not until 1926 that I came into contact with the French Army. At that time I was in the occupied Rhineland as a member of the Rhine Army Intelligence staff stationed at Wiesbaden. I found my

French inadequate and managed to arrange to be sent on six months language leave to improve it. In fact, I went to live *en pension* with a charming French family on the left bank in Paris. This family was horrified to find that the little French I did speak had a German accent, but they set to work systematically to improve it. Grandmother, for example, used to give up her afternoon nap to listen to me reading aloud, a process that it is in my opinion one of the best ways to improve one's fluency.

By the time I returned to Wiesbaden I had learned a great deal about France and the French and had qualified as a First Class Interpreter in the language. What is more, I was able to converse on more equal terms with my fellow French officers and thus cultivate closer relations with them. Perhaps I suffer from certain inhibitions as a result of my northern upbringing, but to me the French have always seemed to have a sort of intellectual éclat which has been denied to the Anglo-Saxon races. In particular, at the time in question, the French officers whom I met seemed to know a good deal more about the military profession and the problem of Germany than I did. I listened to their comments and in my ignorance often felt that they were overestimating the dangers of a German military revival. It was not until I reached the War Office in London in the early 1930s that I realized how justified had been their fears.

Although the occupation of the Rhineland had become a joint Franco–British operation after the withdrawal of the Americans, it failed to bring the French and British armies closer together in concept or structure. Not only were the language difficulties almost insuperable, but the living standards and rates of pay of the British forces were so decidedly superior to those of the French that fraternization and social intercourse were not always easy and sometimes embarrassing. The Germans took every opportunity to exacerbate the differences between the French and the British, although the German authorities often told me that they preferred to deal with the French as the British seemed to find it difficult to make up their minds and give clear direction.

The 1920s and the 1930s were years in which the reputation of the Deuxième Bureau was high. The lessons learned in World War I had been noted, and the tradition had been created that the final victory of 1918 had come about because Foch had been constantly and accurately informed of the strength, effectiveness and positions of the German reserve divisions and the plans of the German high command. The young *aspirants* of the Deuxième Bureau were trained in this atmosphere of confidence, and if it had been possible to penetrate the fastnesses of the Boulevard Saint Germain in 1930 one would have found the staff fully convinced that the outline of future German plans and intentions was known and indeed had been known for some years. In Britain, a belief in the superiority—almost the infallibility—of French Intelligence persisted for many years.

*

French Intelligence in the years between the wars was characterized by certain beliefs and concepts which were very firmly held by the officers of the Deuxième Bureau. Its importance as an aid to decision-making was assumed, yet it was fully accepted that there would often be danger in delaying a decision merely because complete information was not available. In these circumstances, it was the duty of the decision-makers, or the planners, to make provision for the unexpected and to guard against the unknown, while the Intelligence authorities made every effort to fill in the gaps in their knowledge. On the other hand, although Intelligence could not be complete, it had to be as complete as possible; in other words, a commander or decision-maker had to be presented with an estimate (or *synthèse*) embracing all the information relevant to the subject under review. Unrelated scraps of information were dangerous, and those in authority had to be guarded against items which, though interesting in themselves, had not been evaluated and might distort the *synthèse*. As a corollary to this approach, the Deuxième Bureau insisted that its studies should not be confined to purely military matters, but that political and economic factors must be considered part of the work if a satisfactory military *synthèse* was to emerge. The officers of the Bureau were also trained to maintain a healthy scepticism about the reports they received, and to realize that the very best information, even in the form of authenticated documents, is not necessarily a perfect guide to political or military intentions, for circumstances may change and plans may be altered. Such information was, however, worth careful study because it could indicate the general lines of the opponent's thinking at a given moment.

The Bureau sometimes appeared to depend too greatly upon the reports of secret agents and not enough on such things as radio-interception. Occasionally, it seemed to me that it was overwhelmed by masses of contradictory reports from agents of various kinds, and was unable to confirm these reports from other sources. My second reservation is more technical. It results from that certain Cartesian scholasticism with which the French approach all intellectual problems. Applied to Intelligence estimating, these concepts gave rise to a theory of *hypothèses*. First, the situation on the opponent's side was studied in detail, and the known facts established as accurately as was possible. A list was made of all the possible courses of action of which he appeared even remotely to be capable. These were known as *hypothèses*. Further examination was intended to reduce them to a sensible minimum, but no one course was rejected as impracticable unless definite information was available to suggest that the opponent had abandoned it. Those remaining were yet again examined, this time in greater detail, with the ultimate object of arriving at a single course of action which it could be reliably estimated the other side would adopt. Unfortunately such a neat solution was seldom possible, and often French Intelligence officers appeared reluctant to abandon even the most glaring improbabilities except on strictly factual or logical grounds. I do not suggest for one moment that imagination and logic are not vital in effective Intelligence estimating, but even today when I read the works of such French strategists as General Beaufre I occasionally wonder whether the demands of logic cannot sometimes be too rigorous.

Nevertheless, the substantive Intelligence estimates issued by the Deuxième Bureau in the years between the wars, and especially when Gauché was in charge, were outstanding. But although these estimates were given a wide circulation, including political and Foreign Office circles, I got the impression that they did not always reach the highest quarters, namely those where the final decision was made. The Bureau had constantly to fight preconceptions about Germany which were widely held in the senior circles of French officialdom, and it believed that the only way to do this was continually to reiterate the facts. And, as far as the Bureau was concerned, the most important facts were easy to find. *Mein Kampf* was regarded as a clear expression of Hitler's future plans. A good deal of bombast and irrelevance had to be disregarded, but in principle the writing was not only on the wall, but in print. This attitude was in strong contrast to that of much of the British authorities; in Britain the fulminations of *Mein Kampf* were generally regarded by officialdom as having little or no practical value, even as a guide to German thinking, let alone German intentions.

*

The Treaty of Versailles imposed stringent limitations on the German armed forces. In spite of apparent German submission to its terms, French Intelligence remained intensely suspicious of German intentions, an attitude which found little understanding in Britain or America. To them the German request for an armistice in 1918 had merely indicated a temporary pause in German plans. The German Army which returned to the Fatherland in 1918 had been received as an army of victors, and the Deuxième Bureau had no doubt that the Germans would, at a time of their own choosing, make yet another attempt to be victors in fact as well as in spirit. They were not far wrong. Great changes were already taking place beneath the surface in Germany. Secret planning had started as early as 1921, and by the time the able and redoubtable General Hans von Seeckt took charge of the German armed forces in 1923, the small professional army was already showing signs of becoming an élite army of leaders. Only the best recruits were accepted, and for each vacancy there were ten applicants; each member was trained to fill the position immediately superior to the one he then occupied. The military traditions of the old army and the General Staff were revived, jealously guarded and fostered. No new military invention or novel idea concerning strategy or tactics was overlooked by Seeckt and his staff, and opportunities to train abroad with modern weapons—with Russian tanks, for example—were eagerly accepted.

Thus, long before Hitler came to power in 1933, the Deuxième Bureau reported that France was now facing a German Army wholly different in structure and spirit from the force envisaged at Versailles, or for that matter the force defeated in 1918. The divisions still lacked much modern equipment, but the cadres and the trained personnel were available, and German industry was ready for expansion on demand. Once the signal was given it would not be long before a German Army possessing modern weapons was once again a threat to France and the peace of the world. Point was given to this ominous conclusion by Hitler's decision in October 1933 to leave the League of Nations and take no further part in the League's efforts towards disarmament.

In March 1935 Hitler, having formally repudiated the military restrictions of the Treaty of Versailles, jolted international complacency by introducing compulsory military service in Germany. The French were not surprised; it seemed to them a perfectly logical development in the German posture. Quite clearly, German rearmament could not continue at the pace Hitler appeared to be planning unless he could draw on the vast reservoir of manpower which conscription would make available.

In Gauché's view, this was the last moment at which the Allies could have taken successful military action to prevent the further revival of German militarism. In spite of its ominous plans, the German Army was still in the throes of a vast expansion programme, and organizationally was in no condition to take the field. The decision to introduce conscription had come as a surprise to most German senior officers who were still struggling with the problems posed by the creation of new divisions. Many of the most efficient Army officers had been posted into Goering's new Air Force and many of the officers from World War I were proving unsatisfactory. Much of the new equipment, although well conceived, was still in the early stages of development. Heavy divisional artillery and anti-tank units still had to be created, and no single unit of the German Army was completely ready for battle.

In terms of strategic concepts and tactical doctrine, the developments in the German armed forces were corresponding neatly with the Bureau's appreciations. The Panzer divisions, it said in 1935, would reintroduce mobility into warfare, and prevent the occurence of stalemates. They would possess great flexibility and a wide radius of action. They could engage the enemy in battle with great rapidity and achieve surprise at a decisive point. Their mission would be to outflank the enemy and attack his rear, but they could equally be used to penetrate hostile defences, pursue and surround the enemy's forces and destroy them in the field. They were not suited to the holding of the ground they had won, but this task could be performed by the motorized infantry and artillery which would follow them. The Bureau knew that German theoretical exercises were concerned almost exclusively with such wars of movement, in which attacks were directed against the flanks and rear of the enemy and objectives were defined as far as 180 kilometres ahead of advancing troops. The idea of the Blitzkreig was already taking shape and no army without mobile armoured forces could hope to deal with attacks of the kind threatened by the German panzer formations. If these attacks were accompanied by strong air support—of the kind that could be provided by the Air Force that Germany was now developing—they would, Gauché thought, be decisive. While the French Government was considering the action it could or should take when Hitler reoccupied the Rhineland, absorbed Austria or raped Czechoslovakia, it had in its collective possession estimates of this kind prepared by the most competent Intelligence organization in the world at that time.

As the year 1935 drew to a close, Gauché's ideas about the strength of the German forces grew still more disturbing. The tremendous efforts made by the Army and German industry were beginning to show results, even in the short time since conscription had been introduced, and it was by no means clear if Hitler's announced objectives really represented his final goal. Gauché concluded one of his summaries with the words: 'By giving the population a taste of military affairs the rulers of Germany appear to wish to make the idea of war familiar to the minds of the German people.' This was an important comment.

Hitler's reoccupation of the Rhineland in 1936 was the first occasion in modern times on which two military systems of completely different natures confronted one another. German military doctrine was based primarily on an active army of élite and mobile troops, relying little on reserves and capable of surprise attack at short notice. French strategic concepts were still mainly oriented towards the defence of the homeland, and depended upon the mobilization of reserves to provide massive support for the regular forces. A division could require as much as a month to bring it up to war establishment and even then would not have been trained as an entity.

The inevitability of the reoccupation of the Rhineland had been foreseen by the Deuxième Bureau, but, as is so often the case in Intelligence affairs, Gauché had been unable to indicate a precise date when this might happen. This was not surprising, for as little as a year earlier the German General Staff had been planning on the assumption that the

Rhineland would remain forbidden territory to them for some time; when Hitler decided otherwise, he gave no more than two days' notice of his intentions. Commanders and troops were merely told the time and place they were to entrain, and their sealed orders were not opened until some hours after they were on their way and effectively cut off from communication with the general public. Many of the officers thought the whole thing was a training exercise organized by the General Staff to annoy the troops, and left their kits behind. The first time the Rhinelanders knew of it was when aircraft of the new German Air Force appeared overhead.

German troops entered the Rhineland on Saturday, 7 March 1936, and the German military attaché in London appeared at the War Office on the following Monday. He expressed the hope that the arrival of a few German battalions in the old demilitarized zone would not be regarded as a reason for provoking a war. As a result of his discussion the attaché informed his government that in his opinion the chances of war were about fifty-fifty. In fact, the British generals tended to share the Germans' hope that the German action would not be challenged. Where, they asked themselves, were the troops and munitions with which to fight?

In Paris, the German military attaché went to the Deuxième Bureau to express the same hopeful sentiments. After his visit, the Bureau was able to set out for its government a very succinct and important summary of the situation. It was unable at the time to give an exact estimate of the number of troops and aircraft the Germans had employed for the reoccupation, but it considered that the situation was such that a simple threat of military action by France would not be sufficient to cause the Germans to withdraw. Available strength in the whole of Germany was estimated to be about twenty-nine divisions, including three armoured and two cavalry divisions. Although the Germans still had no formal reserve formations, the Deuxième Bureau believed that they could rely on the support of large numbers of paramilitary units, such as the Brownshirts and the Hitler Youth, fanatical groups capable, they thought, of any sacrifice. Even a national rising in defence of the Fatherland on the scale of 1813 could not be ruled out.

The French disposed of some twenty divisions, many of them under strength and poorly equipped, plus the fortress troops in the Maginot Line and some reserves of North African soldiers who were not normally used in France. The attitude of France's allies, with the exception of Poland, was noncommittal, so that France would have to bear the main burden of any action. The Deuxième Bureau was convinced that the only possible military course of action for the French would be an immediate and swift riposte to occupy some important part of German territory, but such an operation could only be carried out by a highly trained striking force in being and ready for action. France, as we have seen, did not possess any such force. French armies might be strong enough to reach the Rhine—in the area of Mainz for example—but with the resources available to them they would be quite unable to cross this obstacle in the face of the sort of opposition to be expected from the Germans; any decisive victory over Germany was therefore just not on the cards; mobilization would take a month and thus any possibility of surprise would be lost. France, in short, had but two options—full-scale war with Germany, or mere political protest.

For a few days—from Saturday until Tuesday—the French decision hung in the balance. General Maurice Gamelin, who had recently replaced General Weygand as French Commander-in-Chief, took a firm line with his government. He said that he could not take action unless he had a million men under arms; further, their transport and some of their equipment would have to be requisitioned from civilian sources, as supplies from Army sources were only adequate for one corps. (General Georges, who was to become prominent in World War II, pointed out rather unhelpfully that according to studies made at Geneva by the League a nation which first authorized civilian requisitioning showed by this very action that it was an aggressor.) Even knowing that she would have little more than moral support from Britain, it looked for a moment as if France would take the risk, but by Tuesday the world was faced with a *fait accompli*. Germany had achieved her objectives. The French decided to be satisfied with a protest to the League.

I do not know to what extent the British Government was aware of the details of the French decision process and the military considerations which entered into it; Britain knew all too little about the French armed forces to express any useful judgement. The Chief of the Imperial General Staff at the time was Field-Marshal Sir Cyril Deverell, a large and clumsy man with but a poor appreciation of political realities; his advice would almost certainly have been similar in principle to that of General Gamelin. In any case, he was soon to be removed because Gamelin thought he was too old for the job.

There did not exist in London any central independent Intelligence organization capable of providing a broadly-based estimate of the situation embracing political, economic and military considerations. Those who knew and those who did not know were hastily called upon for advice; the result was a generalized fear of being dragged into war by the French and, in many quarters, a strong sympathy for the German argument that by reoccupying the Rhineland Germany was only recovering territory to which it had a right.

The Deuxième Bureau drew two main long-term conclusions from the events of March 1936. They were now certain that Hitler was prepared to dispense with the traditional diplomatic preliminaries before engaging in military operations, and any chance that France might have had of forestalling Germany on the Rhine by surprise assault had gone for ever. Secondly, there was now no doubt of the ominous nature of future German intentions; further military adventures were clearly to be expected, and sooner rather than later. However, the Bureau was realistic enough to appreciate that Hitler would need a pause in which to prepare his military forces for his next move.

The shocks of the Rhineland reoccupation passed quite quickly. Austria, having been part of the German Empire in spirit since the disappearance of the Dollfuss régime in 1934, was quietly incorporated in fact by military occupation in March 1938. The Deuxième Bureau had been aware since 1933 that Hitler planned to take it over, but once again could give no date. It was one of the moments when no French Government existed, so that French action was impossible. France's Allies did not consider the formal absorption of Austria, which was in any case a German-speaking state, a cause for European conflict. Once again, however, the Deuxième Bureau was impressed by the ability of the Germans to launch a military operation with a minimum of delay and a maximum of security and, what is more, to bring the operation to a rapid and successful conclusion. To be able to mobilize four divisions and move them 350 kilometres in less than forty-eight hours was in French eyes an astonishing military performance which boded ill for the future. I was a British military attaché in Berlin at the time of the Anschluss, the union of Austria with Germany, and a round of conversations with other attachés from friendly countries convinced me that Czechoslovakia and Poland were next on Hitler's list. The former had not long to wait.

As early as May, just two months after the German success in Austria, the Czech Government, alarmed by reports of the presence of German divisions near her borders, ordered partial mobilization and manned its frontier defences. The true facts concerning these alleged German movements were never accurately established, in spite of a major reconnaissance on the ground and in the air by a group of friendly attachés, of which I was one. The Deuxième Bureau contented itself with the statement that any such concentration would be in accordance with its general reading of German intentions; it added, however, that Germany appeared to need several months to perfect her military preparations before undertaking further adventures, and in particular to complete fortifications in the Rhineland. I remain unconvinced to this day that there were any real concentrations of German troops on the Czech frontier in May 1938, and I suspect that this was also the view of the Deuxième Bureau, although for various quasi-political reasons the Bureau was not prepared to express its opinion directly. But Hitler never forgave the Czechs for this alleged provocation and unknown to the Bureau at the time ordered an increase in the strength of the Army and the Luftwaffe, and gave instructions to press ahead rapidly with the Western fortifications.

As the summer approached, the situation changed with alarming rapidity. Reports of German mobilization were reaching the Deuxième Bureau; one well-placed source claimed to know with absolute certainty that the German General Staff were well advanced with preparations for the military occupation of the Sudetenland. By 19 September the Bureau was able to record with great accuracy the German troop movements towards the Czech frontiers. I carried out a personal reconnaissance of the large military training area of Königsbruck, just north of Dresden, and unearthed what appeared to be unmistakable signs of preparations for military operations. I kept the French military attaché in Berlin, General Didelet, informed of my discoveries, and he informed Gauché.

General Didelet was a pleasant and friendly officer, who had all the social gifts needed by a successful military attaché. He had many contacts amongst senior German officers and great influence with his

own high command. However, in spite of his obvious talents, I sometimes wondered whether he had the military knowledge required to
understand the German situation. My doubts about his capabilities
grew as the events of 1938 and 1939 unfolded, and by the time we all
left Berlin on the outbreak of war it was quite clear that his judgement
had been considerably affected by the events of these years. His
assistant, Commandant Rea, was able and energetic and a very co-
operative colleague; he also had many close contacts with German
officers. When I last heard of him it was rumoured that he had become
a collaborator with the German occupation forces; I find this difficult
to believe.

By 25 August 1938 Gauché had become so convinced of the nature
of the German threat to the Sudetenland that for the first time he felt
himself able to give the French Chief of Staff an unequivocal warning
concerning German intentions. He pointed out that it was most unusual
for an Intelligence officer to be able to issue a warning in such direct
terms. In this he was correct; it is only in the most exceptional circumstances that Intelligence can be absolutely precise in estimates
regarding such things as the timing and plans of their opponents. The
fact that the circumstances of 1938 were exceptional was underlined by
an even more ominous pronouncement by the Deuxième Bureau on
27 September, two days before the Munich Agreement. Germany,
Gauché told his superiors, was not only ready to attack Czechoslovakia,
but was now prepared to face the possibility of world war. The Germans could mobilize 120 divisions, five of them Panzer divisions. The air
force was no less menacing. In August 1938 General Vuillemin, the
Chief of the French Air Staff, had visited Berlin and spent a week being
shown its 'secrets'. He professed himself dumbfounded by what he
saw, although most of the details had already been reported to Paris
by the French attachés. It was nevertheless perhaps unfortunate that he
had gained these gloomy impressions just a few weeks before the
decisions had to be made at Munich, when the Germans boasted that
they had no less than 'two thousand aircraft' on the borders of Czechoslovakia, and that each aircraft had been allotted a military target, an
attack on which would prepare the way for the advancing land forces.
They were ready to lose half of their force to ensure a rapid advance
on the ground. In retrospect it seems unlikely that the Germans were in
fact adequately informed about all potential targets, but nevertheless,

even with smaller forces any planned attacks could have been devasta-
ting, whatever the effectiveness of the Czech anti-aircraft defences.

In spite of their apparent confidence, the German generals did have
some doubts about the capabilities of their forces; these were not
concerned entirely with Czechoslovakia, but with possible French
military reactions elsewhere. Germany had since the spring of 1938
been constructing modern defence lines to protect her western frontier
—the so-called West Wall or Siegfried Line—but these were incomplete.
In fact, at a conference presided over by Hitler at Berchtesgaden just
before the occupation of the Sudetenland, General von Wietersheim,
the Chief of Staff of the Germany army allotted the task of defending
the West Wall, said bluntly that the defences in this area could only
hold out for a short time against determined French attacks. Hitler's
reaction was to remind his generals of their similar fears when he had
occupied the Rhineland in 1936; but he made sure that his plans were
never again discussed in committee by a group of German officers.
When they were together their courage tended to rise and they became,
in Hitler's view, over-critical of his military acumen.

General Wietersheim's estimate may have been right in theory, but
it was quite wrong in fact. Just as the Germans had been mapping the
Maginot Line in detail, the special section established by the French had
progressed far in observing and recording every aspect of the Siegfried
Line. As a result of these studies they had reached the shattering conclusion that it would be necessary to employ the whole of the heavy
artillery available to the French Army to achieve a breach of even a few
kilometres in the first line of the new defences. After this, however,
there would remain insufficient artillery ammunition to continue the
attack. What is more, a study of the alternative possibility of crossing
the Rhine in Alsace where they had a common frontier with Germany
and avoiding the main Siegfried defences had convinced the French
General Staff that any such operation would be impossible with the
reserves available to them. These estimates are of great significance;
they meant that considered French military opinion at the time could
have been responsible for forcing the French Government to discard
the option of resisting German demands at Munich on the grounds that
there was simply no military action they could take or were capable of
to counter German moves or even threaten them realistically. Had he
but known, Hitler was gambling on a certainty.

I was in the Sudetenland at the time of the occupation, acting as a representative of the Ambassadors' Conference in Berlin. Together with an Italian officer, Count Badini, I was responsible for ensuring that the German occupying forces observed the demarcation lines that had been agreed upon at Munich. In the course of my travels in Czechoslovakia I obtained my first real insight into the operation and workings of the new German Army. As an attaché I had attended many Army manœuvres—some of them large-scale exercises—but I had always on these occasions been carefully shepherded by German conducting officers and was rarely allowed to examine any situation or equipment in detail. In the Sudentenland in 1938, however, I was able to wander freely behind the German lines, and I had no doubt about the efficiency of the units I saw. It was obvious that since the occupation of Austria the German forces had made very great technical progress; their equipment was good; their logistical arrangements were adequate; communications and co-operation between the various arms of the service were excellent. All in all, it seemed to me that the Germans were able to field a well-trained, highly-motivated and extremely efficient force.

The propriety or otherwise of the Munich pact has been argued endlessly, and I have no wish to enter the controversy in any detail. For what it is worth, my own view of the situation was based on what I had seen of the effectiveness of the German formations and my own knowledge of the parlous state of British forces at the time. On balance, and on strictly military grounds, I believe that the Munich agreement was justified if—and this is a big if—it was really regarded by those who entered into it on behalf of the West—Chamberlain and Daladier—as a device to give us time to improve our military postures. Remembering the circumstances of the time, I still find it difficult to believe that a serious politician could delude himself that 'peace in our time' was really on the cards.

Gauché had no doubt that from the military point of view it was fully justified. The French choice was either to engage in a war under initially disastrous conditions when neither Britain nor America had rallied to her and when the French forces on the ground and in the air were vastly inferior to the Germans, or to accept a postponement of their challenge, however inglorious.

The French and British Governments have sometimes been

eneral von Moltke, Chief of the
:rman Imperial General Staff in 1914

General von Kluck, commander of the
German First Army in 1914

neral von Bülow, commander of the
rman Second Army in 1914

Lieutenant-Colonel Hentsch, head of
the German Foreign Armies Section in
1914, responsible to General von
Moltke

Brigadier-General Charteris, Haig's Chief Intelligence officer, being greeted
by Queen Mary on a visit to France in 1917

accused of not having made the greatest possible use of Russian co-operation at the time of the Munich pact to deter the Germans. The views of the Deuxième Bureau concerning Soviet military capabilities at that time are therefore of some interest. Briefly, the Bureau believed that, although the revolutionary army had been able to deal with the local revolts that faced it in the early days of the new régime, the Soviet Government had felt itself directly and openly menaced as soon as Hitler came to power because at least part of the living space that Germany claimed she needed lay in Russian territory. In 1933 the Red Army had undergone a vast reorganization, and a considerable part of the nation's industrial capacity was devoted to the production of war material, including tanks and aircraft. The Russian General Staff reappeared, and the number of men in the Soviet forces had risen to over a million and a quarter by 1935. However, this effort was interrupted by the great purge of 1937–8 in the course of which according to the Deuxième Bureau about thirty thousand officers were executed or otherwise eliminated. The effect of this on Soviet capabilities was naturally considerable: colonels commanded divisions and captains were in temporary charge of regiments. The result was that in 1938 the Deuxième Bureau had many reservations about the value of the Russians as a fighting force, and especially about the loyalty and unity of the officer corps and the dependability of many of the troops.

But Gauché was of the opinion that Russia had no intention of interfering in Western affairs, even to save her friends the Czechs. The political conditions she demanded vitiated any effective military co-operation and after a visit to Poland in 1938 he came back convinced that no Russian soldiers would ever be allowed to set foot on Polish soil. Indeed he regretted that the French had told the Russians as much about French mobilisation arrangements as they had.

Whatever the reasons, the Munich agreement was signed at the end of September 1938, and the Sudetenland, the Maginot Line of Czechoslovakia, was immediately occupied by German forces. The world settled down, ostensibly to enjoy the peace, but more realistically to increase defence budgets, dig trenches, and hasten the development of radar, while the Deuxième Bureau noted the new urgency given by the Germans to increasing the efficiency of their mobilization arrangements.

Although the Deuxième Bureau had little doubt that Hitler's ultimate objectives were far from satisfied, it was not until December 1938 that it received the first hard evidence of the likelihood of further German aggression. As a result of this information Gauché addressed a note to his superiors outlining the Bureau's view of how events might develop. He said that French prestige abroad had collapsed and France could not count on finding allies at a critical time. Italy remained faithful to the Axis, while Russian military effectiveness could be discounted. Only Poland remained a potential friend and, threatened as she was on three sides, she would soon be compelled to surrender. With her eastern frontiers secured, Germany could either continue eastwards or turn westwards against France. Her final objective, however, would be Russia and the riches of the Ukraine.

All this proved true, but in those days it was difficult for governments to take any dramatic action on the basis of estimates of impending doom. We are today so impressed by the horrors of a nuclear holocaust that we find it difficult to appreciate the mental atmosphere in which decisions were taken in 1938 and 1939. People and politicians had been conditioned by popular writers and by such films as Wells's *The Shape of Things to Come* to assume that the next world war would mean the end of civilization. Just as many countries today find it difficult to make useful preparations to avoid nuclear catastrophe, so in the late 1930s the politicians of many Western European countries found it difficult to accept the fact that there was a serious possibility of world war or to attribute to the potential enemy any real intention of taking steps which might lead to war. Everyone hoped for the best and confined his efforts to hoping.

Hitler's final dismemberment of Czechoslovakia, the occupation of the Protectorates of Bohemia and Moravia and the creation of the nominally independent state of Slovakia, were forecast by the Deuxième Bureau on the basis of information it received early the same month. There was no military reaction from France and Britain, but from this time a quite surprising change of heart began to take place in these countries. Almost on the spur of the moment Chamberlain guaranteed Poland, now more clearly menaced, but Gauché was not impressed by the guarantee as he knew that Britain had no military forces available to meet it.* Britain began to take an active, even a leading role in

* It is often forgotten that the guarantee extended also to Rumania, Greece and Turkey.

the Franco–British alliance. Steps were taken to increase production of war material, by Britain first and, more reluctantly, by France; the Allies belatedly began to face the harsh facts of German intransigence. In June Britain and France commenced negotiations with Russia in an attempt to give some appearance of reality to the guarantee of Poland. These negotiations were slow and finally completely unsuccessful, but the fact that the French and British Governments were willing to enter into them at all showed a very considerable change of attitude. During these days I was in Berlin and had many conversations with German officers who were determined that Britain should know of the far-reaching military preparations being undertaken in their country. At first these reports were received by the British authorities with a good deal of scepticism—some went so far as to suggest that I was having my leg pulled—but later I was told that my information had played a large part in persuading the British Cabinet to introduce conscription.

In Paris the Deuxième Bureau continued to produce depressing estimates. At the beginning of August the Bureau reported that the German Army was in all respects ready for war, that it had its at disposal some 140 to 150 divisions of which 90 were first-class formations, and that ultimately Germany should be able to field some 250 divisions, or about the same as the maximum number it had been able to mobilize in World War I. In fact, Gauché was greatly overestimating the total number of German divisions. At this time only 98 existed.

It was at this point that the Bureau received a communication from General Didelet, my former French colleague in Berlin. The General advanced the theory that the Germans were in a position to mobilize only a part of their forces and would not be able to realize their total potential in men and material until 1942; consequently, Hitler would not risk war until this date. Didelet's assistant, Commandant Rea, discussed the contents of this very important report with me in Berlin; he was secretive about its sources but he certainly appeared to believe it to be reliable. It is by no means impossible that the information was passed to the French attachés by the Germans, not necessarily to lull French suspicions, but because the German General Staff considered 1942 to be the year when it would be ready to face the consequences of a world war.

I cannot recall that we—the British attachés in Berlin—took any positive action about it other than passing it to higher authority; perhaps we were alert enough to regard it as a possible 'plant'. The Deuxième Bureau, however, was very disturbed by it. The information was of a kind which many French political leaders wanted to hear, for France, politically, economically, and militarily, could wish for nothing better than three years' respite from tension. Nevertheless, the information was contrary to all the Bureau's estimates and General Didelet was formally warned against accepting as a fact information which could at best be only a *hypothèse*. On receipt of this admonition, Didelet changed his tune. He admitted that he had perhaps been too ready to believe unverified information, and said he completely shared the Bureau's view that Germany was preparing to go to war at a moment which best suited her. The Bureau was convinced that Germany had fixed the date for the end of August 1939, but found itself unable, from the information at its disposal, to give a completely unequivocal warning.

★

On the afternoon of 1 September, the day that the Germans attacked Poland, Gauché issued yet another forecast of future possibilities. Never he said, would France enter a war so weak and unprepared. In no single respect was the French Army the equal of the German Army, but French inferiority was most marked in those items which could prove vital—tanks, aircraft and reserve formations. The Bureau did not add—it would perhaps not have been within its terms of reference to do so—but it was nevertheless true, that French political will and military weakness were such that French forces could do little more than squat behind the defences of the Maginot Line. Even in the unlikely event that the French political leaders had been willing to contemplate an active strategy, the state of equipment, the defensive posture and the training of the Army was such that any attempt to force a crossing of the Rhine or to breach the Siegfried Line was unthinkable. For political and moral reasons it was equally impossible to contemplate a violation of the neutrality of Belgium.

It would be unkind to say that this was almost a plea by Gauché that France should remain out of the war. I have much sympathy with him. Although I was in a relatively subordinate position as head of the German section at the War Office I had had at times exactly similar ideas. But I knew that in fact to remain out of the war was impossible.

About this time I paid the first of my periodic visits to the offices of the Deuxième Bureau. I found a general atmosphere of severe depression, which I can now see was at least partly caused by the knowledge of the immense inferiority of the French Army in relation to German forces. Nevertheless, the Bureau could find some comfort in the accuracy of its forecasts, in so far as they related to the Western front. Since 1930 it had never failed to keep its government informed about the facts of German rearmament and growing German military capabilities. On two vital occasions—the Sudetenland crisis and the invasion of Poland—it had provided precise information for its military and political masters. It had resisted the views of those who believed that Hitler was bluffing in the 1930s, and had demonstrated clearly that German foreign policy and military preparations had progressed hand in hand to fulfil Hitler's long-term objectives.

Gauché followed the short Polish campaign with the closest interest. He correctly reported that the bulk of the first-class divisions, including all the Panzer divisions, had been sent against Poland and that to begin with no more than twenty to twenty-five divisions of any value had been left behind to defend the West. But the Polish campaign produced no tactical or strategic surprises for him, nor did the Bureau learn anything more than it had known previously. The German allocation of strength fitted in completely with German strategic principles. The statements Gauché had made about probable German tactics—the use of massed tanks in close co-operation with the air force, for example—were proved correct. He was once again especially impressed by the rapidity with which German units could be brought into action; a unit could be made ready to take the field in a few hours. However, the Bureau pointed out that certain strategic considerations were peculiar to this particular operation and would not necessarily occur elsewhere; these included the absence of frontier fortifications; an enemy not fully mobilized—the Polish Army had begun to mobilize only on 20 August although they had taken some precautionary measures before this late date; the extreme superiority of German forces both in men and equipment; and the opportunity offered to the Germans to advance on broad fronts. Any operations in the West would be of a different character, although there were certain parts of the Western front where similar tactics could be employed. In any case, the lessons of the Polish campaign should be thoroughly studied and absorbed while there was still time. Unfortunately the Bureau's advice was not followed, either in France or in Britain: there was little study of what had happened, and less willingness to draw the right conclusions. In spite of this, Gauché was much criticized—in my opinion quite wrongly—on the grounds that he had not foreseen events more accurately.

Gauché estimated that by the middle of October the bulk of the German forces would have completed their task in Poland, and one of the main issues upon which he had now to form a judgement was whether the Germans would continue their advance towards the south-east—to Hungary, Rumania and Yugoslavia—before turning their attention to the West. He had not long to wait. On 20 September, he received information that large German forces were moving from the East to the West, and by the end of October the Bureau had been able to identify seventy-five to eighty German divisions in the West. At the beginning of November he reported that the German Army was in a position to take the offensive against France two or three days after Hitler made a decision to do so. The problem was to know when and where this hysterical and unpredictable individual would take the plunge.

It was at this point that there came another intervention from General Didelet, who had naturally returned to France from his attaché post in Berlin on the outbreak of war. His argument now ran that Germany would not be strong enough to attack France for at least another year. He therefore believed that the main Allied effort should be made, not on the Western front, but by blockading the Baltic and the Near East; by these means Germany could be brought to heel in a couple of years. In spite of the state of war which existed, Didelet also felt it important that relations between France and Germany should not be completely severed; he even went so far as to suggest that a French mission should be sent to Berlin to observe developments at close quarters as he did not feel that any of the neutral observers would be capable of reporting useful information, or that the secret service would be able to penetrate the extremely efficient German security screen. Some of these ideas were clearly ridiculous, but others were appealing to many Frenchmen. Wishful thinking—that the war would end soon, that it could be ended without vast battles or the long casualty lists of World War I, that it would peter out before it started—remained very prevalent, particularly in France, but also in Britain. Once when addressing a staff conference on the possibilities of a German attack,

Gauché was met by the riposte 'Ah, mon Colonel, ils ne nous ferons pas le plaisir de nous attaquer'. Nevertheless it is only fair to add that neither General Gamelin nor General Georges allowed themselves to be influenced by such sentiments.

In the early days of 1940 it became apparent to Gamelin that he could not control the strategy of the whole war and exercise command over the armies in north-eastern France—the area which would be of crucial importance in any struggle. He therefore appointed General Georges as Commander-in-Chief of the North-East Front, which included the British forces under Lord Gort. Gamelin thus removed himself from control of the key area of the battle, and provided himself with a number of excuses useful for his memoirs. The Deuxième Bureau was divided into two. Gauché remained with Gamelin at his headquarters at Vincennes on the outskirts of Paris, but part of his staff, under his extremely competent assistant, Colonel Baril, was transferred to General Georges's headquarters at La Ferté some twenty miles away. The complications which arose from the need for frequent consultation and the requirement to transfer documents from one location to the other and to obtain the appropriate signatures from officers who were located in the wrong place need only be imagined. In addition, the relationship between Gamelin and his subordinates and the various Air Force commanders and headquarters became equally unsatisfactory. These organizational anomalies were significant but not of overriding importance; it is unlikely that even the most efficient organizational structure could have altered the course of events to any considerable extent. The pattern had been cast in iron by the political decisions of the years between the wars, and no military measures could now alter it.

Nevertheless, the Deuxième Bureau was not only now operating under unexpected organizational difficulty but its sources of information had naturally diminished considerably with the outbreak of hostilities. Apart from a few exceptional agents, it had to rely upon the interrogation of prisoners, the examination of captured documents, and the results of reconnaissance. In the early stages of the war, and in spite of the abortive French effort to mount a minor offensive towards the outposts of the Siegfried Line in the area of the Saar, there was little direct contact between the opposing forces in the West, and thus few prisoners; and unlike World War I, no document of tactical or organizational importance came into French hands. Air reconnaissance, one of the most promising sources of information, was restricted by an extraordinary reluctance on the part of the French Air Force to commit its aircraft and trained pilots to serious reconnaissance sorties. Various excuses were made for this—bad weather, the superiority of the German Air Force, the need to keep good pilots for more modern aircraft, the political undesirability of overflying Belgian territory—but even taken together these factors seem inadequate to account for the failure to engage in operations on which the safety of France could reasonably have been thought to depend. The Bureau consoled itself with Clausewitz's dictum that in any case a large number of the reports one receives in war are contradictory, an even greater number are incorrect and the majority are indefinite, and made the best estimates it could of German dispositions.

Nevertheless, these were surprisingly good. Its tally of German strength in the West in the spring of 1940 was almost exactly correct although it still overestimated the total number of divisions Germany had mobilized and credited the German Army with seven thousand tanks—more than three times the number it actually possessed. However, the Bureau was quite right in supposing that the long winter months had not been wasted by the German High Command as units designated for operations had continued to train, re-equip and receive thorough indoctrination, and it warned correctly that the German Army of 1940 was vastly superior in efficiency to the forces which had been launched against Poland in September 1939.

Gauché now had another task that was as important as calculating the total size and order of battle of the German forces. He had to determine likely German strategy in the forthcoming offensive, and if possible provide a measure of tactical warning of the weight and timing of the attack. This task was exceedingly difficult, for, unknown to Gauché, Hitler and the German High Command were engaged throughout this period in a sometimes acrimonious discussion of their various strategic options—to attack in 1939, to wait until 1940, to attack with the limited objective of separating the British from the French and securing bases for an assault on the United Kingdom, to make a frontal attack across the Meuse, to move swiftly through the Arlon gap in the Ardennes and reach Sedan. These discussions, however, did not prevent Hitler from issuing the alert for troop assemblies almost every time the meteorologists predicted a spell of good weather.

Gauché's task was complicated by a multiplicity of reports, often self-contradictory, which partly resulted from the Germans' own uncertainty and which ranged from the relatively accurate to the plain misleading and quite ridiculous. For example, the series of reports which led to a declaration of a state of alert in the French Army on 12 November 1939 included statements that a revolution had broken out in Belgium and that the Belgian Government had asked for the assistance of German troops. This was perhaps not so fantastic as it at first appears; it was exactly what had happened in Czechoslovakia in 1939. Troop concentrations were reported between Aachen and Luxembourg, and it was said that Hitler had quite recently held an important council of war to discuss an attack on the West.

A second important alert was ordered in January 1940, as the result of reports from Belgium, Holland and Denmark that military operations were imminent. A so-called reliable political source in Italy had stated categorically that Belgium and Holland would be invaded on 15 January. German forces were reported to be arriving in areas close to the Belgian frontiers. Into the atmosphere generated by this combination of conflicting indications broke the news of the forced landing in Belgium of a small German communications aircraft. One of the occupants, a German major, made some dramatic but unsuccessful attempts to destroy the documents he was carrying. When these were examined by the Belgian authorities they clearly indicated that the Germans intended once again to disregard neutrality and to advance through Belgium and Holland into northern France in what seemed like a second Schlieffen Plan. The Belgians, thoroughly alarmed, recalled their forces from leave. Frontier barriers between France and Belgium were removed to permit the passage of French troops who, with the engines of their vehicles running, waited impatiently for the order to cross the border. These orders never came, but the reaction of the Allies had given German Intelligence a valuable insight into many aspects of Allied plans. Gauché considered, however, that he was quite justified in sounding the alarm. On both occasions, the dispositions and concentration of the German forces were such as to enable them to go over to the attack immediately.

Other reports received in early 1940 by the Deuxième Bureau suggested all manner of attacks, from Holland to Switzerland; some said the offensive would come immediately, others that it would be delayed 'indefinitely. One report which was surprisingly near the truth said that the German Army would attack between 8 and 10 May along the entire front from the Swiss frontier to Holland; northern France would be occupied within ten days and the whole of France within a month.

The initiative lay entirely with the Germans, and French Intelligence could do no more than attempt to second-guess German decisions which which might or might not have been taken. Even in the worst circumstances for the attacker it is, or was in those days, by no means impossible to conceal tactical preparations; final dispositions could be delayed until the last moment and troop movements made only at night. In the weeks and months preceding the May offensive the circumstances were ideal from the German point of view: there was still little or no battle contact between the opposing forces, so that the French continued to be denied information from prisoners or patrols or captured documents, and air reconnaissance was at a minimum.

The differences of view about when and where the Germans would erupt extended into the highest government circles. On 9 May, the eve of the Battle of France, at a dinner party given by the American Ambassador in Paris, the French Minister for Armaments and a former Governor of the Bank of France expressed strongly divergent views about the likely course of events. A lively argument took place about whether the Germans would attack in 1940 or postpone operations until later years. The Minister for Armaments believed that there would be no attempt to invade France in the immediate future, and explained that the French armaments programme was based on the assumption that no attack would come until 1941. But the former Governor scoffed at this theory and protested that the German attack could take place at any moment. Those present at the dinner party were disturbed at this clash of opinion on such a vital subject amongst those who might be expected to understand the problem. While the dinner was in progress the German offensive commenced.

The Germans took full advantage of any opportunity to spread every kind of false rumour and report about their intentions, and their security measures were so rigorous that one German division destined to lead the attack through Sedan was not warned until lunchtime on 9 May that it was to enter battle the next day; the chief of operations was on leave, and the divisional commander was preparing for a summer vacation.

Gauché was eventually able to think his way through this mass of conflicting reports and conclude with certainty that the main weight of the German attack would come in the area north of the Moselle River between Limburg and Luxembourg, where nearly all the German Panzer forces were concentrated; from these positions an offensive could be launched at two or three days' notice. He estimated that the Germans would employ 100 to 110 divisions and ten armoured divisions, and this estimate proved to be almost exactly correct. Subsidiary attacks in his view would take place across Belgium and Holland, and in general German tactics would be similar to those they had employed in Poland. There were no signs of impending operations against the Maginot Line, or Switzerland. The operations in Norway had not affected the strength or the equipment status of the German forces, which remained well-equipped, excellently trained, efficiently led, battle-experienced and highly motivated.

There are really very few points on which Gauché can be faulted, and then only somewhat unfairly. First, he credited the Germans with too great a tank strength, though in the end his overestimates were of trivial importance, as the German panzer strength lay more in their organization and tactics than in numbers. The damage had been done years before in 1935 when the French military leaders, like the British, failed to recognize the emergence of the new armoured thinking which derived from British exercises on Salisbury Plain, with its doctrines of speed and mobility. Secondly, he was unable to identify with confidence the German *Schwerpunkt*—the exact centre point of concentration at which the attack would come. This was his most difficult and complex task, and it is highly unlikely that any Intelligence organization would have done better under similar conditions. In fact, in modern conditions of swift movement and radio silences it is doubtful whether a military *Schwerpunkt*, or even its political equivalent, can ever be unequivocally identified in advance when the initiative rests with the opponent. Certainly, we failed to do so in the case of the Battle of the Ardennes in 1944 and, in spite of the most sophisticated assistance, Intelligence has almost without exception failed to give exact warning of Communist political and military initiatives since World War II. To my mind the need for this type of warning represents the greatest challenge to Intelligence officers. Longer-term generalities are often fairly easy to develop; but the provision of precise warning of future events is difficult in the extreme.

Some commentators maintain that the estimates prepared by the Deuxième Bureau in the years between the wars were unduly alarmist. I do not think so. There were some exaggerations and mistakes concerning the details of German strength; Gauché overestimated the total number of divisions that Germany could mobilize. On the other hand, he and his colleagues had thoroughly penetrated German political thinking and military concepts. They realized that whatever the precise strength of the German forces at any given moment, the German people were identifying themselves with the new Army and Air Force, and the whole country was becoming dedicated to a fearsome programme of rearmament. It seems to me that Gauché was quite right in his judgement that it was in 1935, when conscription was introduced in Germany and the German military machine was in a good deal of confusion over its expansion programme, that the West should have taken action to halt Hitler. It is frequently claimed that it would have been possible to put a stop to German ambitions if the West had acted when they occupied the Rhineland a year later, but Gauché argued with conviction at the time that only total war and total mobilization could bring down Hitler. This view seems to have been held by the German generals themselves. By 1936 it was too late.

Although Gauché's estimates were so near the truth, General Gamelin, the Supreme Commander, did not always accept them, and the best estimate is worthless if those in authority do not believe it. Gamelin was a complex individual who was held in no little contempt by the majority of the younger officers of the general staff. His attitudes and reactions were said to be academic rather than military, and he undoubtedly shared the complacency and dogmatism which permeated the higher ranks of the French command structure. He told General Beck when the latter was Chief of Staff of the German Army that it was the duty of every soldier to prevent another war. Such a statement could only create in German minds an impression of a certain lack of resolution on the part of senior French officers, if not of outright French weakness. In spite of the confidence he had reposed in Gauché for many years, his view of the situation in the critical time before the German offensive in the West was often quite different from that of his Intelligence chief. He doubted Gauché's figure for the number of German divisions holding the West Wall and the Upper Rhine and he halved the number of divisions which Gauché estimated the German Army had in reserve. In spite of Gauché's warning about the panzer divisions concentrated in the north, he persisted that German and French deployments in the West were identical, the divisions on both sides being equally distributed along the front. His views about possible German strategy are by no means clear, but he placed the French reserves evenly behind the French front, although Gauché and the Deuxième Bureau were convinced that no attack on the Maginot Line or the Upper Rhine was contemplated by the Germans. Even a German attack through Switzerland seems to have played a part in Gamelin's thinking, for he earmarked French troops to enter Switzerland and support the Swiss Army in such an event. To oversimplify a complex situation, when the Germans burst over us, insufficient troops were available at the right place and the right time to meet it. But the disposition of one's own forces is not a responsibility of Intelligence officers, and Gauché cannot be blamed for these decisions.

The last time I saw Gauché was a day or two before the Germans attacked on 10 May. He presided over our routine liaison meeting with his usual skill. At his side was Colonel Rivet, chief of the French secret service. Premonition of disaster was in the air, but Gauché calmly and with dignity gave one of his masterly expositions of the situation, ending with the words: 'We must now expect a hard battle.' Gauché deserves our thanks for so clearly recognizing that in any Intelligence estimate all the known facts have to be taken into consideration and that this can only be effectively done if one central organization is made responsible for the final picture. In the case of France this could only be the Deuxième Bureau. He warned continuously against the acceptance by those in authority of reports which had not been subjected to examination and co-ordination by the central machine. I believe Gauché to have been a very great Intelligence officer who, faced by the almost insuperable task of trying to get his ideas across to those in authority, never lacked the courage of his convictions. 'Notre Deuxième Bureau et notre S.R. [secret service] ont fait savoir avant la guerre à notre commandemant et à notre gouvernement tout ce qu'ils devaient savoir de l'Allemagne.'* No greater tribute could be paid to Gauché and his work.

....

* 'Before the war our Deuxième Bureau and our secret service kept our High Command and our Government fully informed of all they needed to know about Germany.' Statement by the Public Prosecutor at the Riom trial.

3

GERMANY

In 1927 British troops were still occupying the German Rhineland in accordance with the Treaty of Versailles. I was a member of the Intelligence staff of the British Rhine Army and stationed at Wiesbaden, a spa of great popularity amongst Germans and a favourite place of retirement for German officers. I saw many of them in the smaller restaurants, eking out a frugal existence on pensions cruelly diminished by inflation, yet continuing to maintain considerable dignity. In 1927 Hitler did not yet dominate the German scene, but occasionally so-called 'Brownshirts', members of the Sturmabteilung (SA) of the National Socialist Party (NSDAP), appeared in uniform at party rallies and meetings of various kinds. There were frequent visits to the Rhineland by Nazi leaders such as Goering and Goebbels who were later to become infamous. At that time their main occupation seemed to be to deliver themselves of inflammatory speeches, usually directed against the French rather than the British. We had to take steps to curb these activities, for we could not stand idly by while our allies were insulted.

I was not required to live in barracks, and found myself a billet with a German family in an area known as the Schöne Aussicht, from which, as its name implies, there was a fine view over the town of Wiesbaden. A little higher up the hill was the Ribbentrop villa, rather pretentious, but also with a glorious view. Herr Joachim von Ribbentrop himself was at that time a salesman for a German champagne firm, a position which he is said to have acquired by virtue of his marriage. Certainly there was no indication then of the part he was to play in German history in the years to come. Unfortunately, it was impossible to make any serious social contact with Germans of importance; the officers of the occupation force rarely had anything but the most formal acquaintanceship with the local population. People realized that one day the occupation would end; when that time came, they did not wish to be accused of having consorted with the 'enemy'.

The British occupation ended in 1929, and in 1933 after the Reichstag fire Hitler became Chancellor of Germany. He found himself confronted with generals who were politically conservative and who tended to regard the new Chancellor as an unmilitary upstart. For his part, Hitler considered the officers to be representatives of a rotten and incompetent aristocracy. Nevertheless, they, and only they, could assist him with his plans for the redevelopment of German military strength, for his own Brownshirts were a mere riot squad in comparison with the armed forces—the new Reichswehr. In 1933 and 1934 a continuing battle for power took place between the Army and the Brownshirts; this only came to an end when Hitler had Roehm, the Brownshirt leader, murdered in June 1934. The apparent triumphs of the generals were, however, short-lived. Hindenburg died a few weeks later, and Hitler assumed the title of Führer and the powers of both President and Chancellor of Germany. The Minister of Defence, the generals and every member of the German armed forces had to swear an oath of allegiance to him personally. This oath probably more than anything else prevented many senior generals from joining in any conspiracy to get rid of Hitler. The elimination of Hitler was a prerequisite to any successful plot to overthrow Nazism.

The broad pattern of military Intelligence organization which developed in the German armed forces in the inter-war years was complex and anomalous. At the level of Supreme Command, the Secret Service or Abwehr was directly responsible to Field-Marshal Keitel, the Chief of Staff. The word 'Abwehr' means 'defence', and the name was said to have been given in the hope that Germany's neighbours would be persuaded that the organization was concerned with defence rather than offensive Intelligence. Separate Intelligence organizations existed within the High Commands of the Army, the Navy and the Air Force, but at the time neither Naval nor Air Force Intelligence played any great part in German affairs and decisions. To the General Staff and to Hitler it was the land battles and ground forces which absorbed most of their attention; the naval and air forces of their opponents were seen as auxiliary to these and were left much to themselves. There was also a host of other organizations belonging to the SS, the Foreign Office or to Goering or Himmler which established themselves as Intelligence agencies; it is doubtful if these had any real influence outside their immediate headquarters, but their existence did nothing to clarify the German organizational structure.

The Abwehr was in effect a development of Staff Gruppe IIIb, which had been headed during World War I by the luckless Colonel Nicolai.

In January 1935, however, a naval captain, then forty-seven years old, grey-haired and ruddy-faced, was appointed the Chief. This officer was Walther Wilhelm Canaris, who was later to become an admiral and almost a legend in Intelligence circles, largely because of matters which had little to do with his Intelligence role. When he was first appointed to his responsible post Canaris had no experience at all of Intelligence work, though he was widely travelled and had some knowledge of foreign countries and a gift for languages. He was no stranger to the British, for in 1914 he had been a junior officer in the light cruiser *Dresden*, which had been driven to surrender by the British off the coast of Chile. As a naval Captain, he was an unusual choice to head a staff consisting mainly of Army officers, whose principal task was to obtain information about foreign armies, in a headquarters in which the Army and its general staff officers wielded immense influence. It is said that there was a good deal of hesitation about the appointment in high quarters, and that Canaris finally obtained the job because the Army was short of suitable officers as a result of its rapid expansion.

The Abwehr performed a wide variety of tasks concerned with espionage, 'black' propaganda, political warfare and para-military operations. One branch was charged with liaison between the Supreme Command and the German Foreign Ministry; it received the reports of all German military, naval and air attachés abroad and also, as I know from my personal experience, was responsible for watching the activities of foreign military attachés in Germany. A second branch was responsible for the work of secret agents engaged on military spying, directing their operations, collecting their reports and distributing them to the 'user' Intelligence agencies, principally the Army, Navy and Air Force. A third branch had the task of organizing sabotage and similar irregular operations in the rear of the enemy; for these purposes the Abwehr came to have under command its own so-called 'Brandenburgers', a group of élite commando-type troops, who engaged somewhat unsuccessfully in special operations of various kinds in World War II. To give Canaris his due, he was sceptical of the value of such forces, and realized rightly that their efforts could have little effect on the course of a major war. One of the most important branches of the Abwehr was concerned with counter-espionage and worked closely with the Gestapo in its efforts to identify enemy agents.

Whatever the reasons for Canaris's appointment, once there he

Lieutenant-Colonel (later General) Liss, head of the German Foreign Armies West Section until 1943

Lieutenant-General von Tippelskirch, head of the German Foreign Armies Section until 1941, photographed at the time of his surrender in May 1945

A reconstruction of Marshal Foch presiding over the German surrender to the Allies, in the railway coach at Compiègne in November 1918. On his right Admiral Wemyss, the British First Sea Lord, and on his left General Weygand. The German delegation is headed by Herr Erzberger, accompanied by General Winterfeldt and Count Oberndorff enjoyed Hitler's full support. The funds at his disposal were almost unlimited; amongst other reasons, the Führer is said to have acquired an enormous respect for British Intelligence and was determined to outclass it. Quite apart from his normal duties, Canaris carried out a number of sensitive missions for Hitler personally. When Hitler required Spanish agreement for his planned attack on Gibraltar, it was Canaris who was sent to Madrid in 1941 to make the unsuccessful attempt to negotiate with Spain.

In a sense, it is true that the heads of all national secret services achieve great influence, partly because of the traditional glamour that surrounds the operations of secret agents and spy masters, and partly because of the secret funds at their disposal. Moreover, in addition to the tasks generally allotted to them, secret services can often be useful and influential in promoting unofficial contacts between governments when normal channels have broken down. Canaris was no exception to this rule; the quality of the Abwehr's efforts as an Intelligence agency is a matter of debate, but Canaris himself was for many years a powerful figure in the hierarchy of the Third Reich.

In spite of his power, Canaris remained well liked by the senior military officers. At the time of the Fritsch affair he had been assiduous in collecting information which would help to clear the General of the charges against him; in fact, it appears to have given Canaris a good deal of pleasure to expose the machinations of the Gestapo in this case. The Gestapo never forgot the incident and, when the inevitable battles for power commenced within the structure of the Third Reich, the Gestapo and Himmler's Security Service were only too eager to get their claws into the Abwehr and its Director. In the end, they succeeded; at the beginning of 1944 the Abwehr was taken out of the hands of Canaris and handed over to Himmler. Later, in July 1944, Canaris was arrested for his alleged participation in the plot to assassinate Hitler. He was executed in April 1945, only a few weeks before the end of hostilities in Europe.

A great deal has been written about Canaris's attitude to the Allies, and it has even been suggested or implied that he was an Allied agent throughout most of World War II. I find this difficult to believe, although in the later years of the war when the inevitability of German defeat had become apparent, he certainly made the Abwehr available as a kind of organizational cover for those members of the German

F

armed forces and for others who were opposed to Hitler, and I do not discard the possibility that he may have taken active steps to assist the Allies even earlier than that. In one respect at least the confusion caused by his falling from power unwittingly helped the Allied cause. Early in 1944 Canaris had discovered the text of the radio message that was to be transmitted from Britain shortly before the start of the invasion instructing the French resistance to stand by. The actual message was intercepted by a German Army station when it was transmitted on 4 June 1944, but no action was taken by the Germans. With Canaris in disfavour, apparently no one realized its true significance.

★

The Intelligence organization at the Army High Command was known in the early days of the post-war Reichswehr as the 'Statistical Section' and was formed from the remnants of the Foreign Armies Section, which Colonel Hentsch had headed at the start of World War I. In 1932 the Statistical Section again openly emerged as the Foreign Armies Section (Fremde Heere Abteilung), that is to say the Intelligence section, of the Army High Command.

At first the section was small and insignificant and had available only limited resources. Three regular officers assisted by one or two retired officers were responsible for work on France, Belgium, Holland, Spain and Portugal, while another officer with an assistant attempted to follow the military fortunes of Britain and the United States. Nearly all the officers with Intelligence experience during World War I had disappeared, together with most of their records. There were no handbooks dealing with Intelligence and even the memoirs of Intelligence officers were conspicuous by their absence. It was not until the advent of Hitler in 1933 that the section was able to begin to recruit a larger staff and expand its activities. As time went on, however, the Germans gained a great deal of knowledge about the organization and operation of modern Intelligence agencies from their studies of the practices in use in other countries, and especially in France, for whose Intelligence methods they had great respect. The reoccupation of the Rhineland, the Sudetenland adventure and the absorption of Czechoslovakia not only brought heavy work loads to the Intelligence officers, but also provided them with valuable experience and a considerable amount of factual data from captured archives.

After the occupation of the Sudetenland in 1938, the Foreign Armies Section was rapidly increased in size and importance, and became more formally organized to meet the ever-growing demands being made upon it. Its head was now a General Kurt von Tippelskirch. He controlled two main divisions: Foreign Armies West and Foreign Armies East, as well as the foreign attachés. As their names imply, the former dealt mainly with France, Britain and eventually the United States, while the second was mainly concerned with Intelligence on the Soviet Union.

Generally, German national Intelligence suffered from its complex organizational pattern, and from the absence of any centralized Intelligence structure. Army Intelligence, by far the most efficient part of the organization, was immediately concerned with Intelligence on foreign armies, and to some extent with foreign navies and air forces, but its activities were restricted and it had no power to command the services of the Abwehr, and could only express its wishes through channels that were complex and not always adequate. Canaris was not inaccessible and was ready to receive and consider any criticism of the work and effectiveness of his agents, but he did not permit the Intelligence officers to make direct contact with them. In spite of courses of instruction on military requirements which were arranged for Abwehr officers and a constant exchange of comment and complaint about the detail of reports, the situation remained unsatisfactory. It was, for example, only with great difficulty that Army Intelligence officers came to know what opportunities might be open to the Abwehr's agents, and thus to what tasks it might be worth while to direct their attention. The Germans were not alone in suffering from these problems of communicating with their secret service; similar complications have plagued Intelligence collating and estimating agencies in many countries throughout the history of Intelligence, and seem likely to continue to do so, and they constitute an argument for the American system of combining Intelligence agencies under one head.

The sources of information available to Foreign Armies West were varied. Besides the reports which trickled through from the Abwehr, they included foreign daily papers and technical journals, reports from attachés and information concerning the training and manoeuvres of foreign armies; much of the latter came from the interception of tactical radio links during exercises. The study of foreign military publications, most of which were generally available quite openly to the public, was found to be particularly rewarding. The French *Instruction sur l'Emploi Tactique des Grande Unités*, published in 1936, was available in any bookstore and was read from cover to cover. The British War Office pamphlet on armoured fighting vehicles was translated in its entirety, and was for many years the bible of the emerging German panzer corps. The works of British military writers such as Liddell Hart and Fuller were studied with the greatest care and their lessons eagerly absorbed.

The officers of the Section were required to have more than a passing knowledge of the language of the countries with which they were concerned, and more than a nodding acquaintance with the countries themselves. In a time of great financial stringency in the thirties when few Germans were permitted to use scarce foreign currency for travel abroad, exceptions were made for these Intelligence officers, who could thus increase their professional capabilities. Long assignments on special Intelligence staffs, provided they were interspersed with periods of service with troops, did not have a detrimental effect on the future careers of German officers; when they finally left Intelligence work they could look forward to rewarding employment in command appointments or in other staff areas. Nearly all the officers of the Foreign Armies Section, providing they managed to survive the hazards of the Third Reich, ended up at least as 'Chefs', that is, in the highly responsible positions of chiefs of staff of armies or army groups. This attitude to employment in Intelligence was in marked contrast to that adopted in other countries. In the British Army between the wars, there was not even a Director of Military Intelligence—the job was combined with that of Director of Military Operations—and the 'Charteris affair' left a feeling of uncertainty which did not encourage young officers to volunteer for Intelligence duties.

The officer of Foreign Armies West who was responsible for Intelligence on France, the British Empire and America in the 1930s was Ulrich Liss, who took up his appointment in the so-called Statistical Section as a captain newly qualified from the staff college. With intervals for service with the troops he remained with it twelve years. He eventually became head of the section, and I first met him in

Berlin in the years before World War II. I came to know him very well and found him a most pleasant companion.

Liss, of medium height, fresh complexioned, cheerful and bustling, was in many ways a typical German officer, although he had greater experience and knowledge of the world than many of his contemporaries. Born in 1897 in Mecklenburg, an only child, his father was a distinguished civil official and, rather unusually, the family had no military connections. He went to school in Schewrin, and it was possibly the influence of this garrison town that determined him on a military career. He joined the Army as an artillery officer in 1915, and fought on both the Eastern and Western fronts. After the war he took part in the battles against the communists in the Ruhr, finally joining the Reichswehr in 1921. For the next ten years, incidentally, he was a top-class horseman, winning forty-six major tournament prizes.

He spoke excellent English, as well as French, Spanish and Italian, and he had visited England many times. In 1934 he was attached to the 7th Field Battery, Royal Artillery, where he made many lasting friends.

World War II saw him severely wounded on the Eastern front and while recuperating he went to Paris as a guest of General Speidel. He was there when the Allied landings in Normandy took place on 6 June 1944. Returning to the Eastern front, he was wounded and taken prisoner by the Russians and in 1950 was sentenced to death, but the sentence was commuted and he spent five years in Russian jails before he returned to Germany. It was in Hanover in 1956 that he met Erika von Bülow, whom he married a year later. It was a very happy marriage which lasted until his untimely death in 1968.

Like so many German officers, Liss was an admirer of Britain and the British Empire. He had unconcealed praise for the monarchical tradition and felt himself in some undefined way linked to the way of life and the ideals that he had encountered in the United Kingdom. Both before and after the war he was a keen protagonist of British–German understanding and of improved relationships between Germany and France.

Among Liss's colleagues in the Foreign Armies West in 1938 were the dedicated Nazi, Major von Xylander, who constantly preached the military weakness of France and was later to become a Lieutenant-General, and Colonel Freiherr Alexis von Roenne, who became head of the section when Liss left and who was hanged for his complicity in the plot to destroy Hitler in 1944. It has since been alleged that Roenne deliberately misled Hitler about the Allied landings in France in 1944, so that our troops might have an opportunity to establish themselves ashore. I have doubts about the truth of this story, but it has been linked with the oft-repeated allegation that von Kluge, who in July 1944 had succeeded von Rundstedt as German Commander-in-Chief in the West, made a serious attempt to get into touch with General Eisenhower after the Allied invasion in an effort to surrender his troops to the Allies. Others in the section were Captain Kurnatowski, who died, a major-general, in the notorious Lubianka Prison in Moscow in 1945, and Meyer-Ricks, a young lieutenant who was killed in action in Tunisia in 1943. The names of these officers may not be so well known to the German public as some of the officers who served in German Intelligence before and during World War I and later became famous—the elder Moltke, Graf Schlieffen, Ludendorff, von Einem— but nevertheless they and their estimates had a significant effect on the course of events in the 1930s and afterwards.

Each year until World War II Liss and his colleagues produced a detailed study of French strength and capabilities. The document received only a restricted distribution, and was confined to purely military matters, for Hitler had ordained that political considerations could have no place in a military appreciation. Liss's estimates thus lost some of their usefulness, but they were, within their limits, thorough and complete.

Liss knew that there was a great deal wrong with the French forces. French equipment was obsolescent, if not obsolete, and enthusiasm and drive was lacking in the French armaments industry. It took the French many years to produce a new machine-gun; even the much simpler— and much-needed—new rifle was well behind schedule. The planned expansion of the French Air Force was not being accomplished, and the aircraft it did possess continued to be inferior to those of the Luftwaffe, while anti-aircraft guns were few in number and obsolescent. Liss estimated that it would not be until the summer of 1939 that most French divisions would have new equipment, and even then a major part of the French artillery would still be of World War I vintage.

French strategic doctrine was also known to be obsolescent. The Ecole de Guerre in Paris enjoyed great international prestige, but the

Germans thought it taught an odd combination of strategy and tactics derived from World War I and from the theories of Marshal Foch, the Allied Supreme Commander in 1918. After World War I, Foch had devised a magnificently rational system for the future security of France. Germany was to be 'contained'—though Foch did not use this word in its modern sense, the concept was the same—in both the West and the East. France would be responsible for containment in the West, while Poland, Czechoslovakia, Rumania and Yugoslavia would be France's allies in the East. Foch realized that one day all the nations on the German perimeter would have to defend themselves against a reborn and expansive German state, but in spite of this, or perhaps because of it, he maintained that defence was the most important strategic concept for French forces. Under his tutelage, France came to accept the idea of surrounding herself by fortified lines; if things went wrong her allies in the rest of the world would rally to her aid. Ultimately Germany would be blockaded and in a few years would again be forced to capitulate.

The Army appeared only able to engage in operations that had been thoroughly prepared beforehand; tanks were allowed no independent role but were harnessed to the slow-moving infantry. French officers were taught to advance step by step, as had been the custom in World War I. Strict rules were established about the number of men to be employed on given widths of front, and there was a definite allotment of artillery and ammunition for each situation. Security was the watchword. I remember that teaching at our own British Staff College at the time was very similar. Wing Commander (later Marshal of the Royal Air Force Sir John) Slessor, when he was an instructor there, was one who pointed out the absurdity of these doctrines.

However, an additional important consideration affected Liss's estimates. Aware of the aggressive intentions of Hitler, he tended to emphasize the strengths of the French rather than their weaknesses. He was anxious to avoid superficial judgements which might encourage Hitler during the period when the German Army was in the throes of its expansion programme, or encourage those who wished to hasten a war. Older German officers, too—and especially those who had served in the field against the French—tended to have a high regard for the fighting qualities of the individual French soldier. They rated him as vastly superior to his British, American or Russian counterpart, and believed that he would continue to be tough and intelligent, with a strong sense of patriotic duty. French troops, they noted, fought colonial wars with enthusiasm and devotion and, more, with a clear conscience, convinced that their military efforts were bringing the advantages of French civilization to backward peoples. They would be even more formidable opponents fighting inside their own country.

★

It was against this background that Hitler decided upon his first serious territorial challenge to France and her allies—the reoccupation of the demilitarized Rhineland in March 1936. The advice which Hitler received with regard to the operation was largely negative. German military opinion was convinced that the German armed forces were in no position to wage general war with any hope of success. According to von Manstein, later one of the most successful field-marshals of Hitler's Army, Germany was at the time quite incapable of indulging in the luxury of full-scale war. The German War Minister, von Blomberg, lost his nerve at the last moment; von Neurath, the Foreign Minister, urged Hitler to withdraw his more advanced troops. The Supreme Command waited for news of the French reaction, tense and wary. But France merely ordered a partial mobilization—of about thirteen divisions—and the Supreme Command sighed with relief. There was perhaps a moment when Hitler hesitated over what he himself called his greatest gamble, but when doubters appeared amongst his generals in 1938 and 1939, he was able to quote the Rhineland affair as evidence of his military perspicacity.

There were those few days, discussed in the previous chapter, when the French decision hung in the balance, while General Gamelin claimed that he could not take action unless he had a million men under arms. The Germans had sent some 35,000 well-trained troops into the Rhineland, supported by aircraft, and those who accuse the French and Gamelin of over-caution in an affair which might have been disposed of quickly and competently with a few battalions cannot be aware that even the German generals, who had no real stomach for the adventure, thought that France would have to mobilize her armed forces fully if the situation were to be retrieved.

Although the feeble Western reaction of partial mobilization and a mere appeal to the League of Nations can be justified, the success of the Rhineland operations had a considerable influence on Hitler's military plans. His new self-confidence brought him in conflict with established military opinion, not only over the advisability of future operations, but also over the general lines which German military development should follow. He wished to build up the German forces as rapidly as possible, in order to blackmail the West; in the longer term actual war was already part of his plans, but if he were to wait too long his superiority in modern armaments might be overtaken by the West. The General Staff on the other hand wanted to proceed more slowly, for they were beginning to realize that Hitler's grandiose schemes would eventually require the full reserves of trained man-power and all the munitions that Germany could provide. The General Staff felt that the nation would have done well if by 1942 it had reached a position in which it could meet any aggression with reason-able equanimity and be in a position to undertake foreign adventures.

The hopes of the German General Staff that Hitler would wait before undertaking any new major military adventures were rudely shattered by the absorption of Austria in March 1938. The Generals were given five days' warning of the plan, but the execution of the operation revealed many weaknesses in mobilization arrangements and in the equipment of the forces. Hitler, however, had correctly read the political climate and feared no French interference. Himmler and his so-called Blackshirts (an élite group used by Hitler for special tasks) and Goering and his Luftwaffe took an active part in the occupation. To celebrate the success of their efforts, Himmler and Goering made haste to show themselves to their newly acquired compatriots in Vienna. Hearing of this, von Brauchitsch, the Commander-in-Chief of the Army, became concerned about the Army's prestige and also hurriedly made his way there. On his arrival he was met by Keitel, the Chief of Staff of the Supreme Command, who enquired what on earth Brauchitsch thought the operation had to do with him!

The Sudetenland operation also provided many useful lessons for German Intelligence staffs and they took full advantage of the oppor-tunities offered by their adventures to refine their plans and improve their techniques. Liss's forecast of how the French would react if Ger-many took military action corresponded very closely to the instructions issued by Gamelin. Liss concluded that a slow and methodical advance to the Rhine preceded by mobile forces was the most likely first step.

He was convinced, however, that France would never enter a war unless her Allies were prepared to take the field alongside her. If the British came in they would either join the French reserves or be used to protect air bases in Holland and Belgium.

It was then that General von Wietersheim incurred Hitler's wrath by suggesting that Germany's Western fortifications were in no condition to withstand a determined French attack. Hitler's retort was that there would be no danger if only the generals showed themselves as brave as the ordinary soldier of the line. In the event, Hitler's political acumen was again proved accurate; the operation proceeded according to plan and, as a result of the Munich Agreement, the state of Germany's western defences became irrelevant for the time being.

The Maginot Line fascinated German Intelligence in these years. Liss and his colleagues noted the vital fact that it ended at Sedan and left Belgium and Luxembourg unprotected, and they quickly and accurately summed up its advantages and defects: they believed that it tied down some twenty per cent of French infantry, and recognized its determining and baleful influence on French strategy and its effect on the morale of the French nation which felt itself secure behind this belt of insufficient defences. They systematically set about drawing up a detailed plan of each fort, each major defensive work and each bunker; at the German War College was an exact scale reproduction of the fortifications, and each aspiring staff officer was well grounded in all its details. The information was available to all German troops who took part in the invasion of France in 1940. Finally, the Germans noted that the French took over ten years to construct the Maginot Line—from 1928 to 1939. The German equivalent—the Siegfried Line—was not so complex or sophisticated, but it was completed in eighteen months. But the Maginot Line was more efficient than generally supposed; in 1940 two skilfully mounted and strongly supported attacks by the Germans failed to breach it.

French mobilization plans were supposed to be amongst the most closely guarded secrets of the French nation, and Liss and his colleagues naturally had a professional interest in these details. Largely through an intensive study of how France reacted during the various crises in the years between the wars, and by a close examination of changes in the railway system, they were able to gain an almost exact knowledge of these plans. As a result they followed in detail every step in the mobilization of French forces and could suggest responses which were neither so strong as to be provocative nor so minimal as to be pointless.

After the success of the Sudetenland operation, it was becoming increasingly evident to the members of the German General Staff that Hitler's demands on his neighbours would continue and that eventually the world would lose confidence in his promises and stand and fight. It is by no means clear to what extent Liss was aware of the more complex and technological preparations which were in train, especially in Britain—the development and eventual deployment of radar, for example—but at least it was evident to him that both France and Britain were taking steps to improve the state of readiness and the effectiveness of their forces, and protect their civil populations from the dangers of air attack.

As head of Foreign Armies West, Liss spent part of each year visiting the countries with which he was concerned. In 1938 he was in Paris watching the military parade at Versailles in honour of the visit of King George VI. On his return to Berlin he reported to Hitler that the French troops had made an excellent impression. This was not what Hitler wanted to hear, but Liss who was well aware of the weaknesses in the French Army was pursuing his policy of emphasizing French strength in the now somewhat vain hope of deterring Hitler. It was the first time that Liss had ever briefed Hitler personally; only once more was he to come face to face with him—and that was when Hitler spoke to some of the British prisoners captured in Norway.

In the spring of 1939 Liss was once again examining his estimates. He was now openly saying that the Western Powers would opt for a long war and rely on the gradual mobilization of their military and economic resources to achieve victory. This is the first indication that Liss was beginning to doubt whether an offensive on a grand scale by the Western Allies would ever take place.

During the summer Liss took his usual leave and again set off for Paris, this time to watch the military parade commemorating the revolution of 14 July 1789. It was an impressive occasion. The salute was taken by Generals Gamelin and Georges, who were destined to lead the French forces in war. As a demonstration of solidarity, the British Government had sent contingents of sailors and Guardsmen to the parade, and British aircraft circled overhead. Major Liss (who had received a special travel allowance to permit him to stay in Paris), felt somewhat uneasy about visiting the French capital, especially on such an occasion. French nationalism was strong and anti-Hitler feeling was running high, and the fact that a film entitled *Confessions of a Nazi Spy* was being shown in the French capital was not conducive to the improvement of Franco–German relations. He hoped to slip into the capital unnoticed, for he spoke excellent French and English, and watch the parade quietly and unobtrusively from the crowd. But the European Intelligence community was relatively small, and scarcely had he approached the parade area when he was greeted effusively by a member of the Deuxième Bureau, with whom he was acquainted. 'But Major Liss must have a place of honour from which he can watch the passing troops in comfort and in dignity.' Liss was somewhat taken aback; he would certainly not be able to preserve his incognito, for Colonel Gauché, head of the Deuxième Bureau, was about to procure for him one of the best positions from which to view the proceedings!

Liss had also paid several visits to Italy to see the Italian Army at work, and he reported its many weaknesses. By the spring of 1939 the Germans and Italians had agreed to an exchange of Intelligence and in August Liss was in Italy for the manœuvres of the Italian Army, watching the Italian forces repulse an imaginary French attack in the Alps. Once again he had many reservations about the conduct and outcome of this exercise, but reported that the Italian troops appeared at least able to hold their own.

Later in that same August, while the weather over the whole of Europe continued fine and warm, those echelons of the General Staff responsible for conducting the campaign against Poland moved to their war headquarters at Zossen, about twenty miles from Berlin, and the German troops earmarked to defend Germany's western frontiers against a possible French attack moved out to their positions in and in front of the Siegfried Line.

Liss noted that the atmosphere in Berlin was very unlike the heady days of 1914; there seemed to be little genuine enthusiasm for the coming war, but no one who knew the facts believed that a world war—or at least a general European war—could be avoided. Halder, the Army Chief of Staff, on hearing that the British were joining in, said: 'The British are tough. Now we're in for a long war.' Liss forecast that both France and Britain would support Poland, and he thought that the French could mobilize a total of some 113 divisions or divisional equivalents. The actual number was ninety-nine, but the difference was more apparent than real, for a number of units which he thought would be formed into divisions were in fact used in the Maginot Line. While Liss's estimate of French divisional strength was very near the mark, his estimate of the number of first-line tanks available to the French was grossly inflated, because he insisted on including in the order of battle a large number of tanks which were obsolescent or obsolete. It is curious that both the French and the Germans made the same mistake of overestimating the number of tanks (and aircraft) available to each other.

In spite of many false reports, Liss and the officers of Foreign Armies West were able as we have seen to follow the progress of French mobilization, but their efforts to establish the details of French dispositions were initially hampered by the fact that German troops were forbidden to take any provocative acts in the West by making contact with the enemy or sending land or air reconnaissance patrols across the French frontier. The German secret service had been unable to penetrate French security defences to any significant extent and for weeks not a single agent report had come out of France. Liss knew which French divisions were normally allocated to frontier areas, or at least which divisions had been so allocated at the time of the Munich crisis, and was able to confirm some of this information from the interception of French radio messages. At least it was clear to him that the assignments of senior commanders were identical with those that had taken place a year ago. His first map purporting to show French deployment on 9 September was in fact based almost entirely on what had happened during the Munich crisis. Liss also lacked any information on the movements of British forces, although he was aware that some were arriving in France. The German Army had no long-range reconnaissance aircraft under its immediate control, and it was only after strong representations from Halder that the Army managed to obtain one photograph of the cross-Channel traffic.

However, as the early days of the war passed it became more and more apparent to the Germans that the French were not intending to take any offensive action, even of a limited nature. No French motorized forces had entered Belgium or Luxembourg, though Liss was constantly on the alert for indications that this might be happening, and remained in the closest touch with the German military attaché in

Brussels. Liss stood by his estimate that when French mobilization was complete and the British force had arrived on the Continent there would be some 70 divisions facing Germany in the West, not less than 18 of them mobile divisions and many with tanks. By then Germany would have to oppose this force no more than 36 divisions, only 11 of them first-class and none with a single tank or motorized unit. General von Leeb, who was commanding the troops in the West, was a somewhat apprehensive little man and did not relish the situation at all. He had been brought up in the belief that the French would attack, and it was difficult for him, as an officer of World War I, to comprehend the weakness of the French Army.

Occasional frontier skirmishes took place where French and German troops faced each other, but Liss was astonished to hear French war bulletins speaking of grim battles and fierce artillery duels. He came to the conclusion that this was propaganda to encourage the Poles. No single fact or series of facts produced any firm indications of French intentions. Liaison with Italy, still at this time non-belligerent, about the activities of French troops on the Italian frontier was even less helpful. Hitler, in far-off East Prussia, Brauchitsch, the Commander-in-Chief, and Leeb, his Commander in the West, were all equally confused. After the Belgian Army had mobilized, fears of French entry into Belgium lessened; on the other hand, fears of a French attack against the Saar increased as German Intelligence noted what appeared to be concentrations of French artillery in that area. Little more was known about the British forces; some British officers were said to have been seen in Rheims, Metz and Arras, but there were no clear identifications of formations or units.

The daily routine at the headquarters at Zossen was not unlike that which developed later at Eisenhower's headquarters, except that Zossen was a gloomy and uninviting place where accommodation and food were on a Spartan level. Staff meetings, at first once a day, and later twice daily, were attended by all the principal staff officers, including those from the operational and Intelligence staffs; smaller staff meetings, attended by Brauchitsch (Commander-in-Chief) and Halder, were also held regularly. These opened with a résumé of the available Intelligence, but the operations staffs were secretive about German plans, so that Liss often found himself at a disadvantage.

It was at such a meeting on 27 September 1939 that an astonished assembly of officers, including Liss, first heard from Halder that Hitler had ordered an attack in the West for the beginning of November. Nobody thought that this date could be kept, but an immediate appreciation of the new situation was put in hand. Work on it was interrupted by the unexpected information that the Russians had moved into Poland without warning. This meant that new demarcation lines between German and Russian occupation areas must be hastily devised and agreed. The movement of many of the troops to the West was temporarily halted, and Hitler's demand for an early offensive appeared for a moment slightly irrelevant. Nevertheless, Liss and his staff had to turn all their energies towards preparing for the Western offensive. Whereas their efforts had till now been largely devoted to determining the order of battle and the strategic intentions of their opponents, they had now to concentrate on such matters as enemy defences, widths of rivers and canals, areas that might be flooded, and the hundred and one details of which an advancing army must be aware.

By the time the bulk of German forces had been moved to positions in the West, the situation had began to clarify itself. A variety of sources were beginning to provide more information on the French and their intentions. Radio listening improved. More prisoners were being captured, and although they generally behaved in an exemplary fashion, refusing to divulge any useful information, the impression left by a mass of interrogations was that the morale of the French Army varied considerably from unit to unit and was often less than satisfactory. At the very least it was plain that there was no enthusiasm for an active offensive against Germany. On a more mundane level, German Intelligence officers were able to relate the field post numbers on letters taken from French prisoners to a given unit, and thus the unit to the place to which the letter had been addressed; in this way an order of battle in more detail was gradually built up. One of Gamelin's orders made it clear that he would never sacrifice French lives without ensuring that all 'the requirements for success' had been met. This from the commander who had demanded a million men under arms before he would commence operations against Germany in 1936. How much more would he demand now that he was faced with a vastly superior enemy in 1939? Most importantly, the German cryptographic experts were able to break the cipher used for messages between the French High Command in Paris and the army groups, armies, various authorities within France and the military headquarters in North Africa and Syria. The key to this cipher was changed every four weeks, but the Germans found themselves able to reconstruct it in a few days. The only key which remained inviolate was that introduced on 10 May 1940, and by that time it was of little importance to the Germans whether they read the French messages or not.

By about the end of October 1939, Liss had come to suspect that a good deal of his opponents' inactivity could be laid at the door of the divided command structure and the conflicting interests of the Allies. His understanding of French Army deployment was growing, and his Intelligence summaries began to emphasize the various faults and failings of the Allies and their leadership. Details of the picture were being filled in. A French 250mm anti-tank gun was captured and examined; to the Germans' surprise it was capable of piercing the armour of the majority of the tanks with which the German armoured divisions were equipped, although it appears to have had little effect against German armour when the offensive finally started. A Belgian of German origin deserted and provided a minute and accurate description of the Liège forts. By November, and in spite of the fact that the French had been able to move troops from the inactive Italian front, the weakness of the French Ninth Army in the area between Sedan and Maubeuge was becoming particularly apparent, and it was obvious that once again the French were regarding the Ardennes as an obstacle to any really serious German attack. Air reconnaissance began to provide valuable data; the Belgians were seen to be preparing defensive positions on the River Dyle and building fortifications around Brussels. Captured documents showed that they, like the French, were overestimating the total German strength.

All these details were grist to the German Intelligence mill. Gradually and painstakingly Liss and his subordinates were able to acquire not only the material details of their opponents' deployment, but also that curious conviction (of which all operational Intelligence officers are aware) that they had a full understanding of the enemy's thinking, that they had in a sense been able to enter into the collective mind of the enemy's command and staff.

At the end of November Liss showed his latest order of battle map to Halder. The Chief of Staff immediately and without hesitation put

his finger on the area held by the French Ninth Army and said with
certainty, 'Here is the weak spot. This is where we must attack.'*
Although German Intelligence was never allowed to know a great deal
about operational plans, Liss had heard that the idea of repeating the
Schlieffen Plan and attacking through Belgium and Holland had been
dropped because of the strong opposition it was likely to meet, and
that an opportunity to break through farther south in the Ardennes
area was being sought. This was the first he had heard of the contemplated change. The Commander-in-Chief now arranged for a 'strategic study', a kind of war game without troops, to be held towards the
end of December, and this was clearly intended to test a new plan
said to have been the brainchild of Manstein, although Hitler is known
to have strongly supported it and to have intervened personally in
many of the details. Manstein was at this time Chief of Staff of Army
Group 'A', commanded by Rundstedt, which was destined to deal
the decisive blow in the coming offensive. In this exercise Liss acted as
the Allied commander. There were three courses of action open to the
Allies to meet the German attack. First, they could remain in their
defensive positions or perhaps undertake a limited advance to the
Scheldt; either of these moves would, however, have the disadvantage
of leaving Belgium open to the Germans. Secondly, they could
reinforce the Belgian Army, seize the Albert Canal and take up a
position across the centre of Belgium. Thirdly, they could advance
to the River Dyle in an effort to defend a large part of Belgium; in
the event this is what they did. Whichever of these plans the Allies
adopted (and there seemed no others open to them), it was apparent
that a German attack as envisaged by Manstein in the area of the
Ardennes would meet little serious opposition.

A crucial problem was the disposition of the Allied reserves. Liss had
no firm indications of where these troops were located, but as far as
he could see they were evenly distributed behind the French front,
and not concentrated to defend any particular area, thus indicating the
Allies' uncertainty about German intentions. The possibility of a flank
attack from the south against the projected advance through the
Ardennes was naturally troubling, and Liss was unable to say whether
the French would be able to assemble sufficient forces for this. On

---

* 'Hier ist die schwache Stelle. Hier müssen wir durch.'

balance, he thought they would attempt to do so, even if it meant denuding the Maginot Line, but he did not believe that the units from the Maginot Line could be moved into defensive positions in time to prevent the initial German breakthrough. Incidentally, soon after the completion of this 'strategic study', the Germans received the valuable information that a new French army had been created and given the title of 'Army of Intervention in Belgium'. This was a further clue to Allied intentions, although it is remarkable how few details the Germans were able to discover about the composition of the force itself.

These studies, together with the fact that German forces in the West were improving daily in efficiency as they continued their exercises and re-equipment, had two results. In the first place, the Army High Command became less opposed to Hitler's plans for the coming offensive. Secondly, Liss and his Intelligence staff, sceptical at first, were now completely satisfied that a German attack in the centre was feasible and had every chance of breaking through into open country where the full weight of the German panzers could be brought to bear.

In January 1940 the Germans held another rehearsal of their projected offensive; in this exercise the routes to be followed during the advance through the Ardennes were studied in the greatest detail. In spite of the hard winter weather, excellent air photographs of the Allied defences had been obtained and these were exhaustively examined, and in February a British brigade was identified in the line near Metz.

The Germans, who were nothing if not thorough, held yet another 'strategic study' in March. This was attended by all the chiefs of the operations staffs of all army groups and armies. Liss again represented the enemy. Once again he drew attention to the Allied forces in the north which, he believed, were intended to move into Belgium. He suggested that these forces might attempt to reach the Albert Canal and the Meuse between Liège and Namur, operating in conjunction with the Belgian Army. He described in great detail the weakness of the French forces facing the Ardennes areas where the initial German blow was to fall. He was still in some doubt about the precise role of the British forces, as several options were open to them. But the most inexplicable fact was that the French still retained good quality divisions in the Maginot Line and were not replacing them by troops of lower category. In Liss's view, some ten extra divisions could be made available if the forces in the Maginot Line were handed over to reserve divisions.

By this time Hitler had approved the new German plan in principle, but the strict security precautions which were now observed caused Liss to complain yet again that he was unable properly to evaluate incoming Intelligence in terms of German operational intentions. His complaint was successful and from now on he was kept continuously in the operational picture. The French reserves were still evenly distributed behind the whole length of the front; from this it was evident to the Germans that the Allies had still acquired no firm evidence about the possible location of the German attack. Nevertheless, the question of counterattacks on the flanks of the German advance continued to cause some discussion, though Liss believed that the French High Command was quite incapable of making the rapid, bold and daring decisions which would be necessary if any such counterattack were to be mounted with a chance of success. But he was not able to convince all those present, particularly his chief, von Tippelskirch. Consequently, against his better judgement, he was forced to assume the worst circumstances for the Germans and conclude that they might be faced by a counterattack of some forty divisions. Liss never complained about this, believing that the operations staff were fully justified in taking all precautions, even if Intelligence thought the event highly unlikely.

During the early months of 1940, the state of German knowledge of Allied forces continued to improve. The interception of French messages at all levels had become a most important source, and from the radio traffic between formations Liss was able to deduce the extent that French strength had increased since mobilization. By the end of April, he felt he had identified almost all the Allied divisions and that his knowledge of Allied order of battle was nearly complete: what he did not know, however, was which of these divisions was in the line and which were being held in reserve. More generally, he realized that French morale remained poor, although he still believed that once French soil was invaded the 'spirit of Verdun' would reappear.

There were nearly thirty German alerts during the winter of 1939–40, but the decision to attack, when it came in the early morning of 8 May, was still a surprise to many German commanders. Then it was almost immediately postponed until 10 May because of weather conditions. On one occasion when the generals had asked for a post-ponement because of bad weather, Hitler had sharply commented that the French Army was also not equipped with umbrellas to shield it from the rain. Hitler also felt that any delay in his attack in the West would increase the chances of his plans becoming known to the Allies.

There was a last-minute survey of Intelligence. The Allies were credited with 157 divisions or their equivalents (the actual number was 148), including troops tied down in permanent fortifications such as the Maginot Line and guarding the Swiss and Italian frontiers. The final review of the evidence indicated quite clearly that the German advance would be opposed by ninety-nine of these divisions, plus some reserves and fortress troops. The true figure established from documents captured later in the war proved to be ninety-four divisions in addition to fortress troops. Liss's estimate had been extraordinarily accurate. It should perhaps be added for the record that the Germans had on the decisive front 117 divisions (including ten panzer divisions) out of their total of 136 divisions in the West.

Liss could congratulate himself and his staff. His organization had produced excellent results. He had not overestimated the number of enemy divisions—the traditional error of Intelligence officers. Further, his appreciation of the historical and psychological factors which would affect French and Allied decision-making had been excellent. He had examined and pondered the actions of the French in World War I, he had reviewed French leadership in considerable detail, he had studied French and British textbooks and manuals. Correctly, he and his colleagues had reached the conclusion that militarily France was still living in the era of World War I and that the training and leader-ship of the French armed forces were inadequate for modern war of the kind that the German generals were able to plan. He knew, for example, that Gamelin was obsessed by the fear of a German attack through Switzerland—a fear based partly on information intended by the Germans to reach French ears; what is more, he knew that Gamelin continued to be influenced by this obsession in spite of the fact that the Deuxième Bureau had not been misled. His knowledge of French and British dispositions was such that Halder was able on the basis of the order-of-battle map to establish with confidence the point where the Allies were weakest and where the German *Schwerpunkt* should be concentrated, and he had correctly forecast how the Allied armies would act in Belgium. Finally his understanding of his enemies was such that he was able to dismiss the possibility of an effective French counteroffensive, although even as late as 18 May Hitler was still obsessed with this and had to be shown air photographs of the destruction brought to the French railways to be convinced otherwise.

German Intelligence made only three errors of commission, none of which had any significant effect on the outcome of the battles. Liss credited the French with many more tanks than they actually possessed; the fighting qualities of the individual French soldier were rated too highly by many German officers; and French air strength was over-estimated by the air Intelligence authorities. There was also one important error of omission. The estimates made no mention of the great strides that the British were making in the development of radar—a system which was to prove its effectiveness during the German air attacks on Britain.

Perhaps he may be open to criticism on the grounds that knowing all he did he had not earlier—in 1937 or 1938—come to the conclusion that the French were in no position to carry out major offensive operations in the West.

Strangely enough, Liss always maintained to me that the Allies were better informed about the German forces than the Germans were about the Allies, attributing this largely to the fact that he had no control over the activities of Canaris's secret service. He believed that the occupation of the Rhineland after World War I had provided the French and the British with a magnificent opportunity to set up networks of agents in the area. When the occupation ended and later when Germany reoccupied the Rhineland, these agents could have readily infiltrated the whole of the Reich. He may have been right; I do not know. All I can say is that I saw no signs of the activities of these agents at the beginning of World War II, and my visits to the Deuxième Bureau provided no evidence that the French possessed any sources within Germany which provided information of real value. My own view, to which I shall return in later chapters, is that the importance of the secret agent is vastly overrated in wartime when everything is moving so fast. Ground and air reconnaissance, the interception of radio communications, the interrogation of prisoners of war and deserters, the examination of captured documents of all kinds, patrol activities, contact with resistance groups, the study of newspapers and overt literature and so on—all these sources are vastly more important than spies. Occasionally, of course, an agent acquires an apparently significant document or important information in some other form, but even then it is vital to check it against other evidence before accepting it as truth. One thing Liss did insist on, however, was that no information of any kind should be passed on to higher authority until it had been carefully examined and commented upon by Intelligence.

★

So much for Liss and the officers of Foreign Armies West. We shall next meet him at the Armistice table in the Forest of Compiègne. His colleagues—almost his competitors—in Foreign Armies East were faced with an Intelligence problem of quite different proportions, much more difficult, and one to which the head of Intelligence at Army High Command, General Kurt von Tippelskirch, paid special attention—the study of Russia and its armed forces. I first met Tippelskirch during my service at the War Office in London in the mid-1930s, and I also had some contact with him when I was a British military attaché in Berlin just before World War II, but by this time he was a senior officer and an expert on the French Army and I had little occasion to meet him at all frequently. In appearance he was a short bull-necked man with close-cropped hair, and his demeanour was certainly not impressive. His book on World War II shows great understanding of the British, but I recall him gazing at me through a pair of thin-rimmed spectacles with little charm or friendliness. His aloofness and apparent detachment always puzzled me. Looking back, I now surmise that it was because the British were not for him the principal Intelligence problem. I thought that he appeared to resent his appointment as head of Army Intelligence, which he left in January 1941 to assume command of a division on the Russian front. In 1943 and 1944 he was successively a corps and army commander in the East, and when the war ended he was commanding an army in Mecklenburg, proving himself one of the most competent of German commanders, and later an excellent historian.

There had been a time, in the early 1930s, when German knowledge of Russian forces had been good. This was largely owing to visits by

German senior officers to Russia and to a programme of technical co-operation between the two armies. Russian training manuals were based on German originals and some Russian armaments on German designs. In 1932 Manstein was present at Russian manœuvres. He came away with impressions of abundant hospitality, but low standards of efficiency. The Russians were clearly making progress with the design of arms and the training of their forces, but their staff work seemed to leave a great deal to be desired. The individual soldier was prepared to accept great hardship but the standard of leadership, even junior leadership, was low. Manstein met leading Russian generals and thought that many of them lacked any capacity for independent decision and any willingness to assume responsibility; not that this was to matter, since most of them were to be purged by Stalin. In later years Manstein felt that all the failings he had noted in 1932 were apparent in World War II, and that they accounted for the early Soviet defeats. Nevertheless, the Russians did possess decisive advantages—immense space, plus vast numbers of men and a reasonable sufficiency of equipment for them. Manstein believed that, if Soviet leadership had been without the blemishes he had observed ten years before, the Germans would have met defeat as early as 1943.

Tippelskirch took charge of Intelligence at the Army High Command in 1938. He found that since the period of co-operation in the early thirties Russia had not enjoyed a high priority as a target for German Intelligence efforts, for the Germans did not believe that the Russians had any intention of seeking a war in the near future. Even those who recognized the likelihood that such a conflict might come about at some time in the future did not believe it would occur while Russia was occupied with modernizing her forces and relocating her armaments industry behind the Urals; there were few, if any, who foresaw the possibility that Hitler himself might initiate hostilities against Russia.

The German Intelligence effort was concentrated on potential enemies in the West and Tippelskirch admitted that by 1938 it had become almost impossible to make sensible estimates of Russian military strength. For some years Russia had surrounded herself with an almost impenetrable security curtain. Even when the curtain was drawn aside for a moment, the results were misleading. When foreign attachés were shown elements of the Red Army or the Russian armaments industry, the Russians wittingly or unwittingly appeared to make every effort to denigrate their own efforts. General Köstring who had for many years been German military attaché in Russia, and who had a vast knowledge of its military affairs, told me after World War II that Russia had never put her newest and best equipment on display at any public parade and he instanced the fact that nothing was known about the new Russian tank—the T34—until the Germans met it in action. The Russians issued no White Papers on defence, and no defence estimates. Such figures as they did publish concerning armaments production were in terms of percentage increases over various periods; even if these were accurate they were of little assistance without a firm base. Red Army soldiers carried no regimental or other numbers on their uniforms. Secret agents were notably unsuccessful; any stranger in the Soviet Union, even an innocent tourist, was regarded with suspicion and placed under constant surveillance by the Soviet secret police. The result was that Germany, in common with other Western powers, was induced to underestimate Russian capabilities and potentialities.

Although Intelligence on Russia had only a low priority in the German structure, there was one German staff officer who had interested himself in the subject since as early as 1933, and who later rose to the rank of lieutenant-general, becoming one of the more mysterious figures of World War II and the post-war world. This was Reinhard Gehlen. The details of Gehlen's career are complex and somewhat confused; he served on senior operational and Intelligence staffs and for a time he was head of Foreign Armies East. He was an expert on Russia although he neither spoke the language nor had resided there, although involved in a number of quasi-diplomatic intrigues on behalf of the German Government. He was once presented to Hitler as one of the most brilliant Intelligence officers of the Third Reich, but Hitler seemed to have little appreciation of this revelation. When Guderian showed him a study by Gehlen outlining—correctly, as it proved—the imminence of a Russian attack in a certain sector Hitler remarked that Gehlen should be locked up in an asylum. During World War II Gehlen's reputation and connections with the inner circle enabled him to play a lone hand in the complicated Intelligence manœuvrings within the Third Reich. It is said, for example, that he obtained Hitler's permission to run his own agents in the Soviet

Union, in competition with those of the Abwehr. Eventually, General Gehlen and his organization were captured more or less intact by the American forces in 1945, and their records and archives provided a great deal of the fundamental data upon which further Intelligence work on the Soviet Union was based. With considerable foresight Gehlen had taken steps, while the German forces were being driven out of Russia, to leave in place agents drawn from amongst the Latvian, Lithuanian, Polish, Rumanian and Ukrainian communities. These agents were well-trained and equipped with modern radio transmitters. The Russians were aware of their existence, for Stalin commented upon them to Air Chief Marshal Tedder, Eisenhower's Deputy Supreme Commander, in Moscow in January 1945; on that occasion, in one of his few pronouncements on Intelligence, Stalin emphasized that in his view there was no hope of surprise if enemy agents were permitted to infiltrate effectively, and that the identification and repression of the enemy's espionage apparatus in the rear areas was as essential a part of the preparation for attack as the accumulation of the necessary supplies.

After its capture, the Gehlen Bureau continued to operate in Germany under American tutelage until 1955, when General Gehlen became the first chief of the new Intelligence organization of the Federal Republic of Germany. This was known as BND (Bundesnachrichtendienst), and was located near Munich in southern Germany. General Gehlen retired in 1968 at the age of sixty-six, a small and rarely photographed figure. The air of mystery with which Gehlen surrounded himself has tended to increase his significance and importance in the eyes of the more sensational writers on espionage. A full appreciation of his place in the history of Intelligence must wait until all the facts can be told, but I suspect that his activities were a good deal less esoteric and more conventional and to the point than is generally believed, or possibly than he himself would perhaps admit.

Before considering German Intelligence estimates of Russian strength in 1941, it may be useful to examine the strategic rationale which lay behind Hitler's momentous decision to attack Russia and to undertake Operation 'Barbarossa', as it was called. He was firmly convinced that, in spite of the 1939 agreement, Russia would remain the ideological and political enemy of Germany and would ultimately reveal herself in these true colours. On the other hand, the longer the war with the

West lasted, the greater would be the extent to which Germany became dependent on raw materials which only Russia could supply. When the United States entered the war on the side of the West (and Hitler always believed that this would eventually happen), Germany would have to place still greater reliance on the goodwill of the Russian leaders.

Hitler believed that British strategy was simply to wait until the United States was prepared to enter the war, and Russia turned against Germany. He argued that, if the Russian danger could be eliminated and Russian sources of raw materials acquired in the process, then the continuation of the war against Britain would be simple. Hitler, with his quick successes in Poland and France in mind, had no doubt that German forces could inflict a crushing and rapid defeat upon Russia. He was so sure of the outcome that before the campaign started he had prepared and approved plans for the other campaigns which would follow after operations against Russia had been victoriously concluded in 1941. First would come an offensive in the Middle East which would be completed in 1943 before the United States was ready for combat. Finally, with her rear and her sources of supply secure, Germany could turn to Britain and the West. Liss had given as his opinion that there would be no chance of the Allies invading Europe in 1942 or 1943. So in this respect Hitler could carry out his plans with impunity.

It was in the summer of 1940 that Hitler made the final decision to attack Russia, and in the year that passed between the decision and the attack itself there was little that could be done to improve German perception of Russia and her forces. In common with most observers, including Hitler, Tippelskirch continued to believe that most of the efficient Russian generals and other senior officers had been eliminated in the purges of the thirties, and that consequently the Russian forces lacked leaders with ability and experience. The Germans had followed with close interest the progress of the Russo–Finnish War of 1939–40, and considered that the poor showing of the Russian forces in this conflict confirmed their views that Russian leadership was inadequate. They acknowledged that the individual Russian soldier was hard and tough, but did not believe that he could face modern weapons and tank attacks as practised by the Germans. Neither did the Germans think that the Russians would be able to remedy their failings quickly. The Russians had undoubtedly studied the campaigns in Poland and

France, although it was doubtful if the Russian leaders had been able to profit from this study. But there was a failure by the Germans to realise that the Russian technical and mechanical sense was much greater developed than they supposed.

There were two critical points in the German Intelligence estimates. First, they were inclined to dwell too greatly on the seeming weaknesses of Russian leadership, and to overlook the fact that the Russian soldier could fight magnificently in apparently hopeless defensive situations. Secondly, although the Intelligence estimate of the number of divisions and tanks available to the Red Army was close to the truth, it was clear that these absorbed only a fraction of Russian manpower. There were more than twelve million Russian men of military age, and a major imponderable was the speed with which the Russian authorities would be able to train and arm them. All that the Intelligence estimates could do was emphasize that at all costs the Russian armament industry must be destroyed as rapidly as possible to prevent the production of armaments for these vast reserves of manpower. Finally, there was the Russian weather. Hitler, like Napoleon, had banked on a short spring and summer campaign when the weather would be at its most temperate. Few preparations had been made to provide the clothing and equipment necessary for operations in the fierce cold of a Russian winter.

It has sometimes been alleged that in 1941 Russia failed to heed signs and warnings of the impending German attack. This is not entirely true. On 10 April 1941 Russia declared a state of emergency and increased the state of readiness of the troops on her western frontier. On 1 May she took further measures to improve her defences in that area, while centralized control of the nation was strengthened by Stalin's assumption of full power as Head of Government. The Germans for their part were quite prepared to admit that they had no chance of strategic surprise, and that the Russians would make such preparations to meet an attack as were within their power. The German leaders did, however, hope for tactical surprise, and preserved the strictest security about the timing and place of the intended attack. Whether or not they did achieve this remains an open question. Some Russian front line troops seemed to be expecting the offensive, but the Russian High Command had taken no steps—such as the movement of reserves—which suggested that they had any detailed knowledge of

German plans. Perhaps the Germans were more fortunate in 1941 than in 1942. In December of the latter year a Lieutenant-Colonel Schulze-Boysen, an officer on the Air Force operations staff, and his wife were tried for having betrayed to the West the plans of the German 1942 spring offensive against Russia; it was claimed that the newspapers of the Western Powers had been able to reproduce at least one sentence from the Führer's directive for this attack. In addition, an aircraft carrying a divisional staff officer crashed in no-man's-land on the Eastern Front. The staff officer was captured by the Russians and shot; he was carrying an important order for the German offensive which was to start in a few days' time.

These incidents were in the future when Operation 'Barbarossa' commenced on 22 June 1941. By 4 July Hitler was jubilant. He believed that Russian armour and air force had been annihilated, and was convinced that the Russians could never replace them. Foreign Armies East expressed general agreement with his view. A month later the situation had changed; Hitler was demanding that the developed industrial areas of Russia must be destroyed or captured in an effort to bring about the collapse of the Russian economy, criticizing the Intelligence estimates he had received before the attack, and commenting that the decision to attack would have been considerably more difficult to make if he had been given a full picture of the enemy's potential strength. As the situation stabilized—or, in German terms, deteriorated—comments on the inadequate or misleading Intelligence estimates became more frequent. Goebbels reported in his diary on 10 September, 'The depressing thing is that we have not the faintest idea what Stalin has left in the way of reserves.'

In summary, it is clear that German Intelligence estimates of Russian strength and capabilities in the years immediately before 1941 were entirely unsatisfactory, and for this Tippelskirch must bear the main responsibility. Intelligence is subject to the usual laws for success. If adequate results are to be obtained, all resources must be concentrated on a clearly-defined objective. When the objective was clear, as in the case of France, the results of the German Intelligence effort were brilliant. As far as Russia was concerned, the German Intelligence authorities were undecided until about a year before the attack whether she should be treated as a foe or an ally, and the strenuous efforts which might have penetrated Russian security and provided a more complete and faithful picture of Russian posture and potentialities were not undertaken until it was too late. The failure over Russia demonstrates the major weakness of the German Intelligence structure at this time: the lack of any central directing or co-ordinating agency to undertake forward planning in consultation with the highest levels of the German Government and to direct German Intelligence efforts in accordance with developing priorities. With such central direction more attention might have been given to naval and air Intelligence, especially as the latter was to have such a great influence on campaigns in the West.

The only source of information to which the Supreme Command or for that matter the government had direct access was Canaris's Abwher. As the German armies were forced on the defensive, accurate estimates of the enemy and his strength and intentions became increasingly important. Hitler would sum up a situation by saying that the enemy would soon be at the end of his tether.

It is difficult to determine what Intelligence actually reached Hitler. There were so many organizations vying with one another that it is doubtful whether any fully collated and reasoned appreciations were ever seen by him. Important information was apt to be overlooked in the quarrels about who should pay for it or be its sponsor. Canaris, until his eclipse, no doubt provided those intriguing personal titbits so beloved of spies about the frailties of human nature, but with few exceptions his information does not seem to have been of great value and of course he had other conspiratorial preoccupations which were apt to take his eye off the ball.

Supreme Headquarters had therefore no real central Intelligence organization where reports from all sources could be assembled and evaluated. This was perhaps not so serious in the Russian campaign, which was run by the Army with its own Intelligence section, Foreign Armies East, for some time under the highly efficient General Gehlen. But when Supreme Headquarters was conducting other campaigns, in the West for example, they could at the best expect a once or twice monthly visit from the head of Foreign Armies West, who after all was the expert in the matter. Vainly Supreme Headquarters tried to get the Army Intelligence Staff transferred to it, where it could have formed at least the nucleus of a Central Intelligence Organization but, almost to the very end, the Army Chief of Staff always refused.

4

SURRENDER

In war, the ultimate object of all Military Intelligence activities and operations is victory. Once victory is won, or nearly won, senior Intelligence officers have more often than not found themselves involved in the armistice negotiations which end the wars in which they played their parts. Tippelskirch and Liss were both involved in the Franco–German armistice of 1940. General von Winterfeldt, an ex-military attaché, took part in the 1918 armistice negotiations, and Colonel Hentsch, still seeking to have his name cleared of any responsibility for the disaster of the Marne, just failed by his early death to participate in the armistice negotiations at Brest-Litovsk. I was myself closely concerned with two armistices, the first between the Allies and the Italians in 1943, and the second between the Allies and the Germans two years later.*

There are a number of good reasons why Intelligence officers should be involved in armistices, either on the stage or behind the scenes First, however complete the victory, armistice negotiations are a bargaining situation in which it is of advantage to understand the position of the adversary, and to comprehend his thinking. Normally only Intelligence officers are fully able to do this, and their advice to negotiators both during the drafting of terms before negotiations commence and during the negotiations themselves is invaluable. The Intelligence staffs of the victors usually have a considerable advantage, for their forces have overrun enemy territory and their Intelligence organization is fully operational, while that of the defeated opponent is in disarray. Secondly, there is the practical point that Intelligence staffs usually include amongst their numbers officers who can speak the enemy's language; this ability is in demand both for the 'stage management' of the negotiations and during the meetings. Thirdly, Intelligence often has a major role to play in the post-armistice situation, when the enemy forces must be supervised and disarmed, and it is vital to know the extent to which the terms of the armistice are being observed by the ex-enemy.

For those taking part in them armistice negotiations can be rather

....

* See *Intelligence at the Top* (Cassell, London; Doubleday, New York

dull and prosaic. The representatives of the victors must admit to a certain natural satisfaction in watching a defeated enemy sue for peace; to the soldier this, after all, is what the war has been about. For those on the losing side, armistice negotiations are sometimes appalling occasions. The thought that senior officers can weep is both reassuring and disturbing, but tears are by no means unknown in the conference room: both General Winterfeldt in 1918 and General Jodl in 1945 broke down during the negotiations. I remember that after the instrument of surrender was signed at Rheims on 7 May 1945, Jodl made a short speech expressing the hope that the victors would treat Germany with generosity. I was acting as interpreter and stage manager for the proceedings, but I had not been warned that a speech of this kind might happen. The emotional atmosphere was such that I found some difficulty in adequately translating Jodl's words.

*

On 17 June 1940 the world learned that France had been defeated by Germany, and it was on the afternoon of 20 June 1940 that General Tippelskirch, who had been placed in charge of the arrangements for receiving the defeated French, arrived at Tours in France. He gave orders to the German troops in the area to cease all military operations along twenty kilometres of their front, and at the same time contrived to pass a message to the French on the far bank of the River Loire that the Germans were now ready to commence negotiations on the details of the armistice that the French had requested a few days earlier through the Spanish Government.

Gradually hostilities died down in the Tours area. Tippelskirch awaited the arrival of the French delegation who, it later emerged, were being held up by heavy congestion caused largely by refugee traffic on the roads ahead of the German lines. In the meantime, the Mayor of Tours appeared in full regalia, with his blue, white and red sash across his shoulder, to be ferried across the river to greet Tippelskirch, while the local people produced Champagne and sandwiches to mark their relief that the fighting might soon be over.

It was not until after midnight that the French delegation reached the German lines in some ten vehicles displaying white flags. Tippelskirch had tired of waiting for them and had returned to the headquarters of the Ninth Army at Vendôme. Hastily summoned from his bed, he received the Frenchmen in the street as they stood beside their cars, and the convoy set out for Paris, passing columns of unneeded German troops moving towards the now static front. After a short rest in the capital—a city which Tippelskirch did not know well—the party moved on to the clearing in the Forest of Compiègne, a site filled with memories for both the French and the Germans.

In this same clearing, the Germans had surrendered to the Allies in November 1918. On the morning of 6 November of that extraordinary year, Herr Mathias Erzberger, the German Secretary of State, was informed to his surprise that he was to be in charge of a German delegation which would pass through the German and French lines and seek an armistice. Normally such a delegation would be led by a military officer, and in fact a General von Gündel of the General Staff had been nominated for the task. However, the General Staff was determined that the fact of capitulation should not detract from the image of the military, and that the civilian government should be seen to be responsible; they therefore took steps to ensure that no member of the General Staff was included in the delegation. Erzberger did, however, require a military adviser, and a General von Winterfeldt, a Prussian military figure of the old school and an ex-Intelligence officer who had served as German military attaché in Paris, was brought from the quiet of South Germany to play his role.

When Erzberger reached Spa, the location of German Supreme Headquarters where the delegation was to assemble, there was immediate controversy about its size. For one reason or another some twenty to thirty German officers wanted to join the party. But Erzberger insisted that such numbers were unnecessary and some were politely told to remain behind. Eventually, in the early morning of 7 November, the group left Spa in six motor-cars. Hindenburg was the Supreme Commander of the Central Powers and his final words to Erzberger were, 'God be with you. Get the best terms possible for the Fatherland.' He was relieved that the responsibility would rest on the shoulders of a civilian, and not an Army officer.

Slowly the cavalcade made its way along the Belgian roads, hindered by the unending columns of German troops retreating homewards but, to Hindenberg's credit, retreating in good order. It was well after nine o'clock in the evening when the delegation passed through the German lines and began to fly the white flags of surrender.

The French delegation headed by General Huntziger and escorted by a German officer, on their way to surrender to the Germans at Compiègne in June 1940. The monument commemorating the French victory of 1918 is concealed by the flag of Nazi Germany

The scene in the railway carriage at Compiègne, June 1940. Field-Marshal Keitel is reading the surrender terms. On his right are Hitler and Gœring, on his left Brauchitsch, Schmidt and Hess. The French delegates include, from left to right, Bergeret, Noel and Huntziger

Occasionally a trumpeter blew short blasts to herald their approach. The first French soldiers greeted them with cries of 'Vive la France' and were surprised when the Germans made no response.

At a small town called Tegnier the Germans found a train waiting. They were not told their destination, and as dawn broke they learned from a chance remark that they had halted in the midst of the Forest of Compiègne. Twenty-two years later, the French delegation was equally surprised at the choice of the location for the final surrender.

As they looked from their coaches on the morning of 8 November 1918, the Germans saw a second train on a track not a hundred yards away. This was the headquarters of the Allied Generalissimo, Marshal Foch, and at ten o'clock the German delegation, led by Erzberger, slowly descended from their train and crossed the short distance to the other, the civilians in everyday clothes and the officers in their field-grey uniforms. Erzberger presented his credentials and introduced the members of his party. Marshal Foch, short, perky, and spruce in his new French uniform, formally named his group; it included General Weygand, his Chief of Staff, Admiral Sir A. Wemyss, the British First Sea Lord, looking tired and somewhat bored, and Admiral Hope and Captain Marriott from the Royal Navy, as well as two interpreters. Foch inclined his head slightly and the two groups took their seats at a table in the long narrow carriage, the delegations facing each other. The Germans showed some signs of distress. Just like Admiral Friedeburg at the surrender in 1945, the elderly General Winterfeldt, although outwardly arrogant, could not conceal his feelings. It was a disastrous occasion for him and for the German Army.

Before examining the credentials of the German delegation, Foch asked, 'What do you want of me?' The Germans found this question somewhat disconcerting, and there was a pause before Count Oberndorff blurted that they had come to request the conditions for an armistice. 'I have no conditions to give you,' snapped Foch. 'If you want an armistice, request one formally.' Eventually Weygand, a small, neat figure, read aloud the details of the terms which the Germans were required to accept. The Germans were stunned by their apparent harshness, but were given until 11 a.m. on 11 November to reply. All armistice delegations seem to expect better terms than they get.

Daylight began to fade as the intermittent November rain brought a chill to the scene, and a growing wind blew autumn leaves from the trees of the forest. The Germans pleaded for an extension of time in which to consider their reply, but Foch was unmoved; in any case his hands were tied by decisions already taken by higher Allied political authority, and on military matters Haig had been consulted. The Germans argued that the Allies were encouraging Bolshevism by the extent of their demands; much the same argument was advanced twenty-seven years later by Jodl when he begged Eisenhower's representatives to save as many German troops as possible from falling into the hands of the Russians. In 1945 these representations were brushed aside; in 1918 Foch commented that the threat the Germans saw was not due to communism, but to 'a disease prevailing in eastern armies . . . symptomatic of a nation completely worn out by war.' At one point the Germans went so far as to suggest that the harshness of the terms was intended to invite rejection, so that the Allies could continue the war and occupy Germany. Foch remained adamant; hostilities would continue until the terms were signed. When it was suggested that Foch had treated the Germans with unnecessary harshness, he replied that his attitude had been 'très propre—mais sec'.

The Germans protested against being required to surrender their fleet, which they claimed had never been defeated in battle; Admiral Wemyss told them curtly to bring the fleet out of its safe harbour and see what would happen to it. As far as the Army was concerned, however, Erzberger did gain some concessions which appeared of relatively small significance at the time but which were later to assume great importance: the German Army was allowed to march home with its bands playing and its colours flying. Crowds everywhere welcomed the returning soldiers, and as only the Rhineland was occupied by Allied forces the uninformed in Germany remained unaware or unconvinced that the German Army had been defeated in the field.

While the delegates wrangled in the forest, events inside Germany were moving very rapidly. On 9 November the Kaiser abdicated and left Germany for Holland, while revolutionary fervour was reaching a climax in Berlin. Little of this was known in the West, however. In fact, the French Government and Foch's headquarters were so ignorant of the true state of affairs that when a telegram arrived signed 'REICHS KANZLER SCHLUSS' the French authorities questioned its authenticity, as there was no record of any German statesman with the name of 'Schluss'. 'Schluss' in German telegraphese means 'STOP'.

About 8 p.m. on 10 November a radio message was intercepted saying that the German Government were prepared to accept the conditions of the armistice communicated to them on 8 November, and eventually, during the early hours of 11 November, agreement on details was reached among the delegates. A final meeting was scheduled for 2.15 a.m. in Foch's railway coach. It had already been determined that the armistice should come into force at 11 a.m. and Foch insisted that the final agreement must be complete by 5 a.m., so that warning of the cessation of hostilities could be passed to all concerned. At 5.20 a.m. negotiations were still in progress, so all agreed that they should sign the final page of the long document of thirty-four clauses; when the previous pages had been properly completed the whole document would be dated 5 a.m., 11 November 1918.

At 5.30 everyone rose from the negotiating table. There were no handshakes or other formalities, but Erzberger on behalf of the German delegation harshly declared that many of the terms which Germany had been forced to accept could not be met. He concluded his brief remarks with the heroic phrase, 'A people of seventy millions does not die.' As the Germans left the coach and returned to their own quarters they were unanimous on one point—the deep impression which Foch had made on them during the negotiations. Their German admiration had been evoked by his determination and the rigid formality with which he had conducted the discussions.

There were some in Germany who opposed the idea of an armistice, and thought that Germany should fight on in the hope that somehow or other the situation might improve. One possibility was a spectacular naval action in which the whole German fleet would sail from its refuges to a final victory. Similarly in 1945 there was speculation about, and perhaps even plans for, resistance in a so-called National Redoubt, in the hope that Allied disagreements would lead to a more favourable situation. Generally, however, the need for an armistice was accepted in 1918, although there is no doubt that the surrender left an indelible mark on German national pride; the possibility that some day revenge would be exacted and the memory of these igno-minious hours erased, was never far from German thoughts and plans.

Berlin was in a state of revolution when Erzberger returned to the capital. He received the congratulations of those who realized that he had done his best in a hopeless situation, but others demanded a scapegoat and declared that he had betrayed the Fatherland in its hour of need. He was duly assassinated in 1921.

★

The German sense of humiliation in 1918 must have been heightened by the fact that only a year before they had been negotiating an armistice from a position of strength. On 20 November 1917 the Russians had made a formal application to the German High Command for an immediate armistice with the object of concluding 'a democratic peace without annexations or indemnities'. The frantic efforts of the Western Allies to prevent Russia from seeking a separate peace had failed. From the beginning of October the Bolshevik revolution had been sapping Russian strength and the leaders of the new Russia had come to want peace at almost any price. So on 27 November three blindfolded figures crossed the German lines and were conducted to the headquarters of one General von Hofmeister; these were Russians who had come to make the preliminary arrangements for the negotiations.

The Russians did not find it easy to assemble a suitably representative delegation for the formal negotiations which were to be held at Brest-Litovsk. The leader of the delegation had been recently released from a Siberian prison, and another delegate was a lady who had been serving a seventeen-year sentence for the murder of a former Minister of War. There were a number of uneducated and unaware representatives of the soldiers, sailors and peasants, but the delegation suddenly realized while on its way to Moscow Station en route to Brest-Litovsk that it included no representative of the workers. An old man who happened to be passing by was conscripted for this purpose and distinguished himself at the negotiations by his immense capacity for absorbing alcohol. In addition, there were a number of service officers, including an admiral who was later put to death for his pains.

Brest-Litovsk, except for the small central citadel which had once served as a headquarters for Hindenburg and Ludendorff, had been reduced to a blackened ruin, and the logistic arrangements for the conference were not entirely adequate. For some days, both the victors and the vanquished had to live on half rations. There were also complex problems of protocol. At a formal dinner given by Field-Marshal Prince Leopold of Bavaria, the German Commander-in-Chief in the East, revolutionary etiquette demanded that precedence should be given to the representatives of the people. Thus, to Prince Leopold's surprise, he found a Russian naval rating on his right hand, while the admiral was relegated to a place in an ante-room.

The Germans were prepared to acquiesce in these queer notions, for they too needed peace in the east, and they hoped to settle things quickly, even if not amicably. The armistice terms they had prepared stated quite simply that each side would hold the territory it occupied. The Germans held a great deal, but the bargaining was somewhat more difficult than they had expected, and an armistice agreement was not signed until December 1917. The political negotiations which followed, and which continued until the Treaty of Brest-Litovsk was signed on 3 March 1918, were more difficult still, but Germany achieved almost all her objectives, only to find her efforts nullified by the general armistice of November 1918.

*

So in 1940 the Germans and the French met again in the clearing in the Forest of Compiègne. The same railway coach had been taken from its shelter. Tippelskirch, the man of Intelligence, escorting his party of French delegates, arrived there early in the morning of 21 June, while Brauchitsch, the Commander-in-Chief of the German Army, arrived a little later accompanied by Colonel von Greiffenberg, the Chief of Operations of Supreme Headquarters, and a number of other staff officers including Liss, the head of Foreign Armies West. On their way into the forest the Germans had passed the monument which commemorated the French victory of 1918; now it was discreetly covered and its drooping defeated German eagle and triumphant French inscription were concealed by the flag of Nazi Germany. Brauchitsch had just issued his formal acknowledgement to the members of the General Staff for their share in the victory. 'I thank,' he said, 'all members of the General Staff for the manner in which they have done their duty. True to our traditions we prepared the way for the victory of our troops to whom our hearts and our work are dedicated.' It was quite like old times: the General Staff had come into its own again.

The Germans were aware of the military niceties. The head of the

French delegation, General Huntziger, a native of Alsace, a German speaker, and an experienced field commander, was invited to inspect a guard of honour from Hitler's personal bodyguard. This he did quietly and with such dignity that he was thereafter a respected figure among the German military. He was then led to the famous railway coach. The Press reported at the time that he hesitated and stumbled out of nervousness before entering it. This was not so; he was a rather small man and had some difficulty in mounting the steep steps. Inside the railway coach he found Hitler facing him at the centre of the long narrow table, accompanied by the chief military and political dignitaries of the Third Reich. On his right sat Goering in his exotic Luftwaffe uniform. Keitel, Hitler's Chief of Staff, sat on the other side of his Führer with the terms of the armistice in front of him, and Minister Schmidt of the German Foreign Office acted as interpreter.

There were three main armistices in Europe in World War II; in 1940, in 1943 and in 1945. On each occasion the victors found some difficulty in preparing the draft armistice terms. In 1940, because time was short, the Germans decided to use the 1918 armistice terms as a model. In May, Hitler, carried away by the overwhelming military successes of the German forces, had said rhetorically that it would only be necessary to demand the return to Germany of all that she had lost in the past four hundred years. This was a fine idea from Hitler's point of view, but the details were more difficult, and real work on them did not commence until almost too late. In the end Keitel personally took a hand in drafting the terms, and the preamble is said to have been written by Hitler himself. Mussolini had to be informed, even though he had only declared war on France on 10 June. Hitler finally met him and gave him the details of the terms, emphasizing the fact that he had no intention of demanding the surrender of the French fleet, for if he did it would certainly join the British. Hitler made it quite clear that Mussolini would not be invited to take part in the negotiation or signature of the main German armistice. The French would of course have to sign a separate armistice with Italy.

Hitler had two main preoccupations in the preparation of the armistice terms and the conduct of the negotiations in 1940. In the first place, he wanted to be sure that nothing in the terms presented to the French would jeopardize the rapid ending of hostilities. They must be sufficiently restrictive to prevent any possible future military threat from the French, but must not be so harsh as to provoke any serious reaction at a time when Hitler knew he would be engaged in a struggle on his Eastern front; if it were possible, it would be best if the terms were such as to win a measure of French co-operation. Perhaps, thought Hitler, this magnanimity would be modified later when the question of a formal Peace Treaty arose; this Treaty might well see the imposition of more onerous terms. In the short run, however, the ending of the battle in France and the security of the Western front were all-important.

Secondly, it must be seen by all the world that the humiliation of 1918 had been revenged. This was why the Forest of Compiègne had been chosen for the ceremony, and why the preamble to the terms presented to the French stated quite bluntly that it was the German intention to erase the shame which had been imposed on the German people, and to make good the injustice which had been done to them.

In the railway coach, Keitel opened the proceedings at 3 p.m. by saying, 'I must pay homage to the valour of the French soldier and honour the memory of all on both sides who shed their blood for their countries. It is an honour for the victor to salute the vanquished.' Germans seem to make statements of this kind readily and without embarrassment; they do not come so easily to the British or Americans. Keitel then read out the detailed terms. General Huntziger listened carefully. The French fleet was to be spared the humiliation of surrender, but the Germans had not forgotten the severe restrictions which had been placed upon their own Army in 1918; the French Army was to suffer a similar fate, and be reduced to minimal proportions. All arms and warlike stores not needed for the tiny force would be handed over to the Germans. As soon as the terms had been read Hitler abruptly left the coach with his aides, and Jodl took his place on one side of Keitel with the head of the operations branch of Supreme Command on the other. The French asked for an hour's recess to study the terms, and withdrew to a tent which had been erected in the clearing.

They tried valiantly to moderate the terms and to win time to discuss them with Pétain who, they said, must make the final decision. In particular Huntziger made a brave attempt to protect the refugees of various nationalities who had sought asylum from the Nazi régime in France, but the Germans were adamant on this point. Without exception, these persons must be handed over to the German authorities.

Certain concessions were made concerning the French Air Force, but in the end Huntziger advised Pétain that Keitel's attitude was un-compromising and that further concessions were unlikely. The Ger-mans, incidentally, had in any case taken steps to intercept the telephone conversations between Huntziger and his demoralized government in Bordeaux. The negotiations dragged on until 22 June, when at 5 p.m. Keitel delivered an ultimatum and demanded an answer one hour later. There were further delays and approaches by the French, probably inspired by Pétain, but, after a final warning by Keitel that he would break off negotiations, Huntziger said a few minutes after 6 p.m. that he was ready to sign the armistice. When he had done so he reported undramatically by telephone to Pétain in accepted military phraseol-ogy: 'C'est fait, mon genéral.' Keitel signed on behalf of Hitler; five years later in Berlin he was to sign a document of a totally different nature—the unconditional surrender of the German armed forces.

The armistice could not come into force until a corresponding agreement had been reached with Italy. This condition deeply shocked the French. They had been defeated in the field by the Germans, but the Italian troops had only penetrated the French frontier at a few points, and that after the Franco–German armistice. Many of the Germans, who had come to admire and respect Huntziger for the soldierly way in which he had conducted himself during the negotia-tions, had a good deal of sympathy with this point of view. Liss and some of his colleagues remembered an estimate of the Italian Army and its probable combat efficiency which Foreign Armies West had issued in 1939. This had been so uncomplimentary to the Italians that Hitler had ordered it to be withdrawn from circulation immediately; there were some things one could not say about a friend and ally. Nevertheless, the requirement for a meeting with the Italians were inescapable and Huntziger flew to Rome, escorted by a German Intelligence officer, and accompanied by General Marras, the Italian military attaché to Germany whom I had known in Berlin just before the outbreak of hostilities, and who had always seemed to me to harbour very friendly feelings for the British.

The Germans celebrated their victory with a military drum tattoo, followed by the hymn 'Nun danket alle Gott' ('Now thank we all our God'). Hitler joyfully danced a few steps and then with a few World War I cronies paid a visit to the old battlefields nearby. The following day he and Keitel enlisted the services of a guide, toured the sights of Paris, and visited the tomb of Napoleon. The idea of a large-scale victory parade through the city was abandoned, as Goering would not guarantee it immunity from air attack. Brauchitsch, who had never been in Paris, took the opportunity to fly low over the city with Liss, who pointed out to him the main places of interest. On the deserted streets they saw no French traffic, but only German military vehicles.

In Rome the Italians raised no serious objections to the armistice terms, although, rightly as it turned out, they had some concern about the absence of any clauses concerning the future of France's North African colonies. The agreement with the Italians was signed on 24 June, and six hours later, just after 12.35 a.m. on 25 June, the agreement came into force simultaneously on all fronts. The main armistice commission set up its headquarters at Wiesbaden, the lovely *Kurort* where I had spent so many happy days in the years between the wars. Liss was to have one final satisfaction. When the French produced all the relevant documents he found that they agreed almost exactly with his own calculations.

Although humbled militarily, France had not been entirely disgraced. Six French divisions of the Army of the Alps, their rear threatened by German forces, had held at bay thirty Italian divisions. The troops holding the Maginot Line had refused to surrender until they received a direct order to do so, although they were within the grip of the encircling panzers. France still had half a million men under arms in her colonies and possessions, and many of these were to join the Allied cause and continue the battle against Germany, although no arrangements were made to transfer troops from France to North Africa for this purpose. But the French, like the Germans, had to have an immediate scapegoat for the apparent humiliation they had suffered, and the kind and precise Huntziger, who had now become Commander-in-Chief of the French Army, was subjected to a great deal of criticism from his fellow countrymen on account of his seemingly close relations with the Germans, and the ostentatious way in which he later entertained in his villa on the outskirts of Vichy; according to his detractors he failed to show proper regret for the events in which he had played so important a part. In 1941 he was killed in an aircraft accident in France.

★

The stories of the Allied armistices with the Italians in 1943 and with the Germans two years later have been told many times; my own part in them is described in some detail in my book *Intelligence at the Top*. All I wish to do here is to add some footnotes to history.

Neither in 1943 nor in 1945 did the Allied powers have ready a suitable document with which to confront their opponents. Events had taken us by surprise, and there had been great difficulty in obtaining agreement amongst the Allies on the details of the proposed documents, and reaching a reasonable concensus between the political and military authorities. In the case of the Italian armistice, for instance, General Eisenhower, who was in charge of operations in the Mediterranean theatre, wanted a brief and pointed document, which would be sufficiently acceptable to the Italians to bring about a rapid agreement; Eisenhower's main interest was that the armistice should readily lead to Italian assistance in the continuing campaign against the German forces in Italy. In foreign policy and political circles in London and Washington, on the other hand, there was a desire for a longer and more formal document which would represent a testament to the total defeat of Fascism. In the case of the German armistice, complications arose because no one had taken steps to ensure that Eisenhower was in possession of the draft terms suggested by the European Advisory Commission which had been sitting in London and on which Britain, the United States, the Soviet Union, and later France were represented. In the absence of this draft, Eisenhower was forced to prepare his own terms for the initial surrender, and it has always seemed to me that the Russians must have been surprised if not suspicious that the conditions of surrender they had helped so carefully to prepare were not used.

A remarkable thing at this time was the feeling among many senior German officers that Germany would do best by placing its future in the hands of the Russians rather than the Allies. They argued that the superior potential of Russia offered a better outlook for Germany. Admiral Dönitz, Hitler's successor as head of State, considered such views monstrously shortsighted and he strongly opposed the idea that the German fleet should sail to Kronstaat in Russia. This was not the least of Dönitz's problems. In the last days of the battle for Berlin Hitler had delegated to subordinate commanders the right to award decorations and effect promotions. It had led to a glorious spree in which Jodl for his services was allotted the highly prized 'Oak Leaves'.

But Keitel put an end to all this and turned his attention to what to do with the pictures of Hitler displayed in public buildings. For three days this thorny problem was debated until it was decided that they should be taken down only in rooms when official meetings with the victors took place. But already some disillusionment with the Allies was apparent. Field-Marshal Busch reported that 'negotiations with Montgomery were exorbitantly bad and dishonourable. The British', he said, 'instead of rebuilding were retarding—they worked slowly, bureaucratically, and little.'

The ending of most modern wars has been accompanied by fears among the victors that armistice negotiations will run into difficulties if they are taken out of the hands of military men, and if an attempt is made to inject too great a political content into what is the essentially practical matter of ending hostilities and saving lives on a field of battle. This was true in 1918, when President Wilson of the United States tended to confuse the intention and significance of the armistice with that of the following Peace Treaty; the military authorities were determined that the armistice negotiations should be left to Foch, and that political and economic matters should be dealt with later at a formal peace conference. In Italy in 1943, Eisenhower expressed exactly similar fears, and to make the position quite clear he instructed General Bedell Smith, his Chief of Staff and chief negotiator, to inform the Italians that the armistice would be concluded between Eisenhower (represented by Bedell Smith), acting on behalf of the Allied Combined Chiefs of Staff, and the Italian High Command, and not between the governments of the Allied nations and the Italian Government. In 1945, too, Eisenhower was anxious that the negotiations for the unconditional surrender of the German armed forces should not be prolonged by political discussion. Rightly or wrongly, military leaders are generally fearful that negotiations on political conditions, once entered upon, will prolong the war and lead to senseless loss of life, or that the continuation of operations during the negotiations will make it necessary to retain in the theatre military forces that may be needed elsewhere. Certainly in 1945 Eisenhower was aware of the requirement for United States forces in the Pacific and the Far East, and was determined to release troops from the European theatre as soon as possible.

Compared with the most recent examples of armistice negotiations —those concerned with the ending of the wars in Korea and

Vietnam—the armistices in 1943 and 1945 were concluded with startling rapidity. The difference of course is that in 1943 and 1945 the Allies were negotiating with the representatives of powers which, even if they had not been finally defeated in the field, were very close to collapse. It is extraordinarily hard to impose an armistice, and especially a humiliating armistice, on an opponent who retains the capability and the will to fight. In many senses, the negotiations at Panmunjon and between the Americans and Hanoi in Paris were, and are, not armistice negotiations at all; they represent political bargaining conducted against a complex background in which the wars to which they relate are merely single factors.

This is equally true of the American–Soviet attempts as I write to bring about an armistice in the Arab–Israeli fighting—attempts complicated by the fact that the Arab guerrilla leaders can afford to ignore some of the political realities that must be heeded by rulers of national states, and by the unworldliness of the Israeli right-wingers. This, with its accompanying spread of violence to countries remote from the main theatre of action, is yet another example of the complicating effect on local wars of the reluctance of the super-powers to be brought into contact with one another; still greater since Russia's big increase in strategic nuclear weapons.

With the striking increase in mass communications in recent years, notably television, one means of pursuing victory in the wars we have seen during this period has been the undermining of the public will to continue the fighting on the other side. The absence of a clearcut military victory has been a feature of all these wars and this being the case a cease-fire agreement could only be reached after the leadership on one side or another has decided that its public opinion would stand no more. Hence, in my view, a difficulty of concluding armistices or cease-fires under conditions so greatly changed from those which have been given most consideration in these pages. The assessment of public morale is a most formidable aspect of these and poses quite new problems for Intelligence. The existence of vast nuclear arsenals invalidates most of the ideas about power, compulsion and defeat on which people of my generation were nurtured.

It is another reminder of the need for Intelligence chiefs to remain alert to the changed appearance of problems.

5

BRITAIN AND THE UNITED STATES

The latter years of the World War II and the beginning of the post-war period were in a sense the golden age of British Intelligence. It was not until the middle or late fifties that the unlimited resources of the Americans began to make their weight felt in the increasing excellence of the work of the CIA. Now there is no doubt of American pre-eminence in a field that is becoming increasingly technological and professional, and increasingly dependent upon the willingness of governments to invest large sums of money in highly skilled personnel and expensive equipment.

British Intelligence has for long had a reputation—sometimes justified and sometimes not—for wisdom and efficiency. Sir Francis Walsingham, the Secretary of State to Queen Elizabeth I, is said to have been a master of the techniques of espionage. At one point he enlisted the services of the most gifted Oxford and Cambridge graduates, sending them to study in France in an effort to penetrate the secrets of the French court and thus learn of French designs against England. He also made a practice of intercepting foreign and domestic correspondence, reading it covertly and then despatching it on its way to its unwitting recipient. Oliver Cromwell placed a Secretary of State named Thurloe in charge of Intelligence, but, presumably in the absence of adequate facilities for security vetting, Thurloe appointed as his assistant a gentleman who promptly became what is now called a double agent, and passed information about English Intelligence and Cromwell's plans and policies to his enemies; some claim that it was through the intervention of Thurloe's assistant that King Charles II was able to avoid a number of somewhat clumsy attempts upon his life. In those days—and indeed until the nineteenth and twentieth centuries—the political and economic problems that faced the dominant powers were relatively uncomplicated and could be satisfactorily surveyed by a national leader with a small group of advisers. In these circumstances Intelligence needed merely to provide items of information; elaborate organizations to collate these items and form judgements on them were not required.

In the years between World War I and World War II, when the international situation had become very much more complex, the main task of Intelligence was to watch events in Germany, and to provide warning of any developments there that might be threatening to the interests of peace. Other tasks—Italy, Russia, Japan, even France—were subsidiary to the main mission, though each presented its own problems. It proved surprisingly difficult to form an opinion about Italy and the Italian armed forces; whether this resulted from an awareness of the need for security on the part of Italian officers and officials, or whether it was merely due to the fact that few of them knew anything of interest, I cannot say.

In some ways our ally, France, presented the most difficult problem of all. French ambitions and intentions were always a subject of controversy in British circles, and the efforts to provide explicit information about them were not particularly successful. At one point two British officers who were well known to the French, were sent to France to take up minor business and industrial appointments; the hope seems to have been that they might come across useful information, or at least make useful contacts. The authorities in London were rather aggrieved when the French felt themselves unable to overlook their presence any longer and arrested them on charges of espionage. Thereafter there was tacit agreement that there should be no further spying against France.

In general, British attachés in Paris were compelled to spend so much of their time in social activities that they could see little of the French armed forces. British officers attached to units and formations rarely witnessed any serious military activities and had neither time not opportunity to form valid opinions on French military efficiency. The British, like the Germans, tended to think of the French only in terms of their techniques and successes in World War I.

In spite of the small staff that was available, the effort directed towards Germany was a good deal more serious, and met with varying success. In the years before World War II great reliance was placed on the activities of attachés in Germany and officers sent on attachments to the German armed forces. The sources of information of these attachés were almost entirely overt. Careful scanning of the local press, and then perhaps a weekend visit to a given area in an attempt to confirm a press report; checks of the shoulder and collar badges of servicemen on leave; careful observation at, say, a naval launching ceremony; items from conversations at social gatherings; visits to manœuvres and to army exercises: all these bits of data added up to useful pictures in the minds of competent attachés.

There were, as far as I know, no secret agents to purloin plans from the German Supreme Command, or to produce a ready made time-table of German intentions, although there were plenty of rumours to keep everyone busy. Indeed, unless there had been a traitor in Hitler's immediate entourage able to transmit information on the Führer's varying moods and decisions, I doubt whether any secret agent would have been particularly useful. As far as the German Army was con-cerned—and the Army was the main strategic instrument of German policy—we were reasonably well informed in general terms; con-sidering the size of the problem we were perhaps better informed than we had been at the start of World War I. Good information was also available about the German Air Force, an enterprising assistant air attaché, Wing Commander Coope, had submitted a series of penetrat-ing and well-documented reports. Information on the German Navy seemed harder to come by, and we knew much less about naval affairs. The main trouble in London, however, was not an absence of data but the lack of any system for the central study and analysis of attaché and other reports and the absence of effective co-ordinated arrange-ments by which considered and well-documented studies of German military expansion could be presented to the government. Each service presented its own estimate, tailored to its own ideas and preconcep-tions of where Germany was going, and sometimes tailored also to its own budgetary requirements. The lack of a central structure was even more apparent in the early efforts to correlate political, economic and military information in order to reach an agreed view of Hitler's general strategy and to determine what limitations existed on his ability to realize his global ambitions. So many alarming and contra-dictory reports were being received—one reaching London at Easter 1939 claimed that a bombing attack on the Home Fleet was imminent —that further but not very successful attempts were made to co-ordinate unchecked and ungraded information and to scotch rumours that were often an embarrassment to the government.

At the outbreak of World War II, this problem of co-ordination had become acute and apparent, and the authorities had come to realize that the British Intelligence structure was in a state of considerable disarray. In spite of Coope's excellent reports it appeared to the government that available information on the strength of the German Air Force was less than satisfactory, and that some warning of the advent and importance of the dive-bomber should have been possible; it seemed that German tactics with tanks and aircraft had come as an unjustified surprise. Yet nearly all this information was available in London in one form or another. The trouble was that there did not exist adequate machinery to get the information to the people who really mattered or to sift the mass of available facts, rumours and opinions relating to the political and military aspects of the current situation, and to draw from this material considered judgements in terms that were likely to be useful in the decision process. Nor was there any great inclination in many quarters to face up to unpalatable facts, especially if they were contrary to established policies.

It is true that a committee had been set up just before the war for this kind of purpose, although even in 1940 no one seemed to understand its functions or have any ideas about the process by which it should perform its role. The committee, known as the Joint Intelligence Committee, was nominally subordinate to the Chiefs of Staff, and was chaired by a representative of the Foreign Office. It included amongst its members the heads of the Intelligence departments of the three armed services—a vice-admiral, a major-general, and an air vice-marshal. Once war had started the committee met each day at 3 p.m. in a room in the Cabinet Offices in Great George Street in London. Its members produced titbits of information on subjects they felt should be of interest. These were often unrelated and sometimes contradictory, and the secretary was left to put them into some sort of order for general distribution. It was not until much later that the Committee had its own expert joint staff capable of making considered preliminary assessments. There was no attempt at continuous or evolving study, and no effort to cover current events in a systematic way. In other words, the committee served no useful purpose either as an estimating staff, or as a staff to handle current Intelligence.

A separate group which was formed with the more clearly defined task of reviewing Intelligence relating to the prospect of a German invasion of the United Kingdom performed much more satisfactorily, and produced a series of relevant and useful summaries concerning the invasion problem. On the other hand, the handling of Intelligence relating to the Norwegian operation left much to be desired. This

'Bill' Cavendish-Bentinck, chairman of the British Joint Intelligence Committee, 1939–45

John A. McCone, Allen Dulles's successor as Director of US Central Intelligence

Allen Dulles, Director of United States Central Intelligence, with President Kennedy, visiting the new CIA building outside Washington. Behind the President is Robert S. McNamara, the then Secretary of Defense

United States Intelligence Board, March 1966. From left to right: Lieutenant-General Alva R. Fitch, Defense Intelligence Agency; Charles H. Reichardt, Atomic Energy Commission; William O. Cregar, Federal Bureau of Investigation; Edward Proctor, Central Intelligence Agency; Richard Helms, Deputy Director of Central Intelligence, and later Director; James S. Lay, Executive Secretary; W. F. Raborn, Director of Central Intelligence, Chairman of USIB; Sir Kenneth Strong; Thomas L. Hughes, Department of State; Lieutenant-General Marshall S. Carter, National Security Agency; Major-General John J. Davis, US Army; Rear-Admiral Rufus L. Taylor, US Navy; Major-General Jack E. Thomas, US Air Force tragic adventure was controlled directly by a ministerial committee presided over by Winston Churchill, at that time the political head of the Admiralty. Such was the desire for secrecy that the plans were not discussed with the Intelligence community. No Intelligence estimates of the strength of the forces the Germans might be able to bring to bear were requested, nor any judgement on possible German reactions to an attempt to prevent the movement of iron ore from Narvik to Germany. I believe that if a properly co-ordinated Intelligence appreciation had been available, this farcical expedition would never have taken place.

The obsession of operational planners with secrecy—a constantly recurring factor through the history of Intelligence—can be justified to some extent, but it seems to me that it goes to quite ridiculous lengths when it is used to justify the exclusion of appropriate members of the Intelligence community from participation in the planning process. I find it difficult to understand how any plan can be made in the absence of a professional assessment of an opponent's strength, capabilities and intentions. The Norwegian campaign was neither the first nor the last example of this extraordinary syndrome in Britain, and other countries have not been free from it. It may be argued that the publicity given to Philby and men like him casts doubts upon the discretion and security of those engaged in Intelligence. But the Intelligence community has a greater interest in secrecy and security, when these can be justified, than has any other branch of the staff. In any case, I am convinced that the Philbys of this world are much less important individuals than the claims made for them would suggest. If the junior cashier of a bank absconds with the cash, it is annoying and possibly detrimental to the bank's affairs, but it does not mean that the whole banking system is about to collapse. I am aware that in the case of Philby it has been suggested that he was likely to become the head of the British secret service, but I do not believe that there was ever the slightest chance that this would occur.

*

Thus, when Bill Cavendish-Bentinck came upon the scene in October 1939 the British Intelligence community was confused and seeking leadership. This leadership was to be Cavendish-Bentinck's greatest contribution to British Intelligence in particular, and to the war effort in general.

Cavendish-Bentinck had been rejected by the Army at the age of eighteen as too tall and too thin, and his first contact with the Foreign Office was in 1915 when he served as an honorary attaché at the British Legation in Oslo. This was not at all to his taste in wartime, and he again attempted to join the Army. This time he was successful and he served in the Grenadier Guards for the remainder of World War I. After the war he returned to the diplomatic service, and held increasingly important appointments in Warsaw, Paris, The Hague, Athens and Chile. By 1940 he had become a Counsellor and was clearly marked for further promotion within the diplomatic service. When he assumed his appointment in the Intelligence community he had had no previous experience in the field. He was faced with a choice of the Intelligence appointment or the headship of the important Egyptian and African Department in the Foreign Office. He chose the former as he felt it was likely to give him more scope and to be more interesting.

Once at his new desk, he quickly observed that the arrangements for the co-ordination of planning and operations were working smoothly and efficiently, and had been doing so for some three or four years. The members of that other branch of government, the joint planning staffs, were generally officers of high calibre who had a broad knowledge of government machinery in Whitehall. In the absence of any effective centralized arrangements for the provision of Intelligence, they had been forced, on the relatively rare occasions when they felt a need for information, to consult departments individually. Naturally they received conflicting views, and thus had come to doubt the usefulness of the information they received and to rely to a greater or lesser extent upon their own intuitive judgements. This was partly their own fault as they had refused to have the Joint Intelligence Committee representatives sitting in a room next to them. As they were officers of experience, their judgements were often reasonably wise, or at least not wildly inaccurate, but this amateurish system was no substitute for a fully professional and co-ordinated structure. Cavendish-Bentinck was not slow to realize that if Intelligence were to perform a useful function and play its right role in the war effort, it would be necessary to develop the structure on the lines of the successful planning organization.

The committee over which Cavendish-Bentinck found himself presiding in 1940 was a group of individualists. Rear-Admiral John Godfrey, the Director of Naval Intelligence, had inherited the traditional mantle of British Naval Intelligence, with its air of superiority over the Army and the Air Force; he tended to regard those who differed from the views of the Navy as recalcitrant sailors who must be severely dealt with. He was undoubtedly the dominant personality among the three service directors of Intelligence and was a master of the 'broad brush' or sweeping generalization; seldom did a problem present itself as wholly maritime, but any disposition to ignore the affects of seapower upon it was smartly dealt with. His colleagues were clever men of great detail—a common tendency at least in Army staff officers. The two attitudes, the general and the particular—or perhaps the admiral and the particular—did not blend easily. What is more, the civilian representative of the Ministry of Economic Warfare who was also a member of the committee was regarded as a kind of interloper; certainly, his carefully prepared estimates received little attention unless they fitted in with the preconceived ideas of at least one other member of the committee. The diplomatic ability of Cavendish-Bentinck was bound to be tested. In retrospect, the most unlikely feature of the structure was the fact that the three service Intelligence chiefs were prepared to subject themselves to the chairmanship of a non-service diplomat with no previous experience in Intelligence. But there were obviously great advantages in having a chairman with a wide range of political experience and close contacts with the Foreign Office. In any case, there was no real alternative, since none of the service directors was prepared to serve under the chairmanship of a service colleague.

Bill Bentinck was a man of erect figure and pleasing presence, with a somewhat military appearance. He had a sharp and incisive mind which readily grasped detail. He was very well-informed, and appeared to have access to many sources of information; he had a curious habit when disclosing a new item of referring to his source in a way which defied all penetration. He had a multitude of acquaintances in all walks of life, and a talent for listening sympathetically and mentally recording all he heard. His new colleagues found that he was an excellent chairman, tactful, relaxed and good-tempered; he would lean back in his chair with his hands pressed together and listen, looking very wise and cunning, and keeping the discussion to the point.

Eventually he would intervene in a slightly bantering manner which would remove the heat from really contentious issues. He had the scepticism that any good Intelligence officer needs, and a mental alertness which usually put him that vital step ahead of the other members of his committee.

Here I wish to concentrate upon three major questions which were of paramount importance for the strategy of World War II. With the advantage of hindsight the decisions taken by Cavendish-Bentinck and his committee on these issues may appear fairly simple and obvious; in the circumstances of the time, however, they were complex and difficult in the extreme. It is impossible to assess with any precision the extent of Cavendish-Bentinck's personal participation in these decisions, for he had a tendency to bring his influence to bear somewhat indirectly, while his service colleagues argued more loudly and openly. To my mind, however, there is no doubt that without Cavendish-Bentinck's unobtrusive guidance the British Intelligence structure—and thus the total war effort—would have operated at a considerable disadvantage.

The first of these issues was concerned with the invasion of the United Kingdom. After the fall of France and the evacuation from Dunkirk, Britain had a breathing space of which it made full use to improve its military posture and equipment. The possibility of an invasion remained uppermost in British minds, although it began to loom less large as the results of the great air battles with the Germans became known. It was then that Cavendish-Bentinck took his first important decision. In October 1940 his committee reported quite firmly that in its view an invasion of the United Kingdom was no longer likely. There had been a considerable controversy in the committee before this view was accepted. Both the Navy and the Air Force representatives produced evidence about naval strengths, invasion craft, and the weakness of the German air force to back the contention that the possibility no longer existed, but the Army member maintained that anyone who believed the Germans would not invade was a lunatic. Cavendish-Bentinck himself was convinced that the Germans would not make an attempt at invasion unless they had complete air superiority over the Channel—a condition which they seemed less and less likely to attain as the summer of 1940 wore on. Eventually, as the signs of German activity and preparations diminished, the last fears vanished and Cavendish-Bentinck was able to present a unanimous verdict to the Chiefs of Staff.

Many in Britain could not bring themselves to accept this estimate without reservations, although it was expressed quite unequivocally. The estimate, we now know, was accurate, for by the middle of 1940 Hitler had decided to direct his next attack upon Russia. Nevertheless, the invasion of Britain did remain in Hitler's mind, for in January 1941 he told Admiral Raeder that once the Russians had been conquered it would be possible to deal with the British under much more favourable conditions. I remember having to appear later in 1941 before a group which was examining this problem. I was certainly not prepared to give it as my opinion that the Germans had abandoned the idea of invasion for all time, although it was apparent that the operation had been at least postponed.

As the prospect of invasion faded, Cavendish-Bentinck turned his mind to the next German move. Reports had begun to appear that the Germans were contemplating an attack on Gibraltar, with the co-operation of the Spanish Government. Cavendish-Bentinck's committee made a very thorough examination of this prospect in the last weeks of 1940, and came firmly to the conclusion that Franco would not co-operate with the Germans, and that the Germans would not enter Spain without his co-operation. This was an important conclusion with far-reaching implications for British, and eventually Allied, strategy. The committee's estimate was accurate, in the sense that Germany did not attack Gibraltar. However, the capture of Gibraltar did figure in German plans as late as June 1941.

Under Cavendish-Bentinck and with the sympathetic advice and support of General Ismay (later Lord Ismay), the secretary of the Chiefs of Staff, the committee gradually and steadily grew in authority. It is true that Cavendish-Bentinck himself was not reporting personally to the Prime Minister, although the latter examined his appreciations most carefully, but from the middle of 1941 all members of the committee were regularly invited to attend Chiefs of Staff meetings and give their advice, which was at least listened to. These meetings were often difficult as the Chairman of the Chiefs of Staff Committee, Field-Marshal Sir Alan Brooke, was frequently very sceptical of the Intelligence estimates, particularly those produced by the Navy and the Air Force, and had a habit of gobbling like an infuriated turkey when he disagreed with anyone's remarks. He firmly believed that the Army produced the best Intelligence officers, but he was not allowed to have his own way, for the Navy argued that because of the dangers and unpredictability of the sea, even in peacetime, the naval officer was the more realistic in his estimates. These attitudes persist even today in certain circles. Naturally, the Chiefs of Staff were at liberty to reject the advice of the Intelligence officers, and often did so, but there was no challenge to Cavendish-Bentinck's position as chairman, and this in itself was a great tribute to his tact and ability. Nevertheless, although the situation was improving, it was still a long way from the ideal of an inter-departmental committee to control Intelligence, with an independent chairman divorced from any department and responsible directly to the Prime Minister. Intelligence still remained a field in which all men were experts, and it required the arrival of Eisenhower and the Americans to demonstrate that, if battles were to be won, Intelligence must have a position of true professional authority in the staff and organizational structure.

The third important estimate made by Cavendish-Bentinck concerned German intentions towards Russia. In February 1941 he reached the conclusion that Russia was the next German objective, and this view was formally expressed by the committee in March 1941. Cavendish-Bentinck had personally become convinced that this estimate was accurate because good reports, chiefly from Polish sources, had suggested that the Germans were enlarging their airfields in Poland and strengthening the runways. In addition, a report was received from Turkey that the Germans in that country had begun to subsidize anti-Soviet activities in the Caucasus and the Crimea, and there were many other indications of German intention. Churchill is on record as stating that Cavendish-Bentinck's committee was slow to appreciate that the Germans would next turn their attention to Russia, but this is not correct. As soon as the evidence became clear and the matter became more than a 'hunch', Cavendish-Bentinck persuaded his colleagues to make a firm judgement on the issue, and by April their ideas were beginning to be accepted. However, on one important point Cavendish-Bentinck differed from his colleagues. He thought that the German invasion would end in failure, while some other members of the committee felt that the Russians would last less than six weeks. I know of only one other person who thought at the time that the Russians would survive; this was Admiral Mountbatten, who openly expressed the view that Hitler would never defeat Russia and that the débâcle of 1812 would be repeated. He pointed out that Hitler should have launched his attack earlier in the year, and added that in his view the enthusiasm of the Nazi forces would evaporate once they realized that they had no hope of victory. While estimates on Europe and Africa had been outstandingly good, the same did not apply to South-East Asia. Cavendish-Bentinck felt that the disasters there were to some extent due to faulty Intelligence. He realized that not enough attention had been given to this area, and Intelligence resources which might have been switched to the East after 1941 were still kept fully occupied by events in the West. But in this Britain was not alone as the tragic events at Pearl Harbor so amply demonstrated.

It is difficult to compare Cavendish-Bentinck with the other senior men of Intelligence of World War II, for none of his contemporaries had the power and responsibility that came his way. Gauché was an admirable technician but had no great influence on those in high places; Tippelskirch never aspired to be more than a competent evaluator of the enemy's forces. In America, Dulles had yet to arrive on the Washington scene. Canaris in Germany was an intriguer; as we have seen he was for most of the war the only Intelligence authority at the German Supreme Command, but he was still mainly concerned with his secret operations. Thus Cavendish-Bentinck became the first Intelligence officer in any country to have a reasonable measure of co-ordination over all Intelligence activities; and it is surprising that this arrangement came to pass in Britain, a country addicted to government by committee and averse to centralized authority. Admittedly, Cavendish-Bentinck's powers were in no way comparable to those later given to the Directors of Central Intelligence in Washington, but nevertheless he was able, because of his diplomatic training and innate ability, to assume sufficient authority to bring the British Intelligence machine to a state of real efficiency.

Cavendish-Bentinck's general views of Intelligence were ahead of his time in a number of ways. In the first place, he discovered that many junior officers in the service ministries were duplicating each other's work, and foresaw the need for a centralized system. He urged the establishment of a Joint Intelligence Bureau in London to deal with certain non-military matters, and matters that were the concern of more than one military service. After a good deal of opposition this came about at the end of the war, and many years later the three service directorates of Intelligence were integrated with the Joint Intelligence Bureau in one Intelligence division at the Ministry of Defence. Arrangements for centralized estimating were also further developed and the position of chairman of the Joint Intelligence Committee was consolidated as the pivot round which the whole structure revolved.

Secondly, he had a healthy understanding of the limitations of secret agents. He realized that unless they were in the highest positions in their own countries they were unlikely to obtain any particularly useful information, and that whatever their claims, their reports should be confirmed from other sources. He appreciated, however, that these activities must continue, both because other countries engaged in them and because of the chance that information of vital interest might emerge. He also realised the fact that Intelligence had often lost in authority because of the extreme secrecy which surrounds its activities. Naturally a great deal of information must be classified, but one cannot hope that there will be proper support for Intelligence if so many facets of its work are concealed. Cavendish-Bentinck did much to make the nature of his responsibilities known to as wide an official circle as possible. Much of the secrecy which attaches to Intelligence arises from the need to protect the affairs of those employed in the secret services, and this is obviously necessary. What is not so sensible is to allow this aura of secrecy to spill over into matters which are in much less need of protection.

Thirdly, Cavendish-Bentinck was one of those who understood the importance of the United States in world affairs and in the field of Intelligence. I remember him visiting Eisenhower's Supreme Head-quarters in 1945. My military assistant at the time was Kenneth Keith (later Sir Kenneth Keith), an officer who was later to reach great eminence in the City of London. He took Cavendish-Bentinck on a tour of the front to visit the headquarters of Generals Omar Bradley and George Patton; such operational headquarters are invariably sur-rounded by thick mud, through which Cavendish-Bentinck was forced to pick his way in his smart London suit, wielding his neatly-rolled umbrella. During this visit Cavendish-Bentinck was everywhere received with great kindness and hospitality, and subjected to typically efficient American briefings. When he had completed the tour he was more than ever convinced of the importance to the Western world of the immense military strength and potential of the United States; above all, he hoped that the Soviet leaders would come to appreciate the true implications of United States resources. After Pearl Harbor he had put his experience in British Intelligence unreservedly at the disposal of the Americans, and he now urged the creation of a central agency for intelligence in the United States in the hope that the Americans could avoid the competition between competing interests which had flourished in Britain.

Cavendish-Bentinck's services to the Intelligence community were rewarded with promotion within the foreign service while he continued to serve as chairman of the committee and, at the end of World War II in 1945, with the post of British Ambassador to Poland. After his retirement from the diplomatic service in 1947, he became prominent in industry, serving on the boards of several British and German public companies. Perhaps the best tribute that can be paid to his work in Intelligence is to point out that when, at the end of the war, the British Government was being forced to make economies, the Chiefs of Staff believed that whatever reductions might be made in the armed forces budgets, the Intelligence structure should remain intact. Such a judgement would have been unthinkable before the era of Cavendish-Bentinck.

★

I first met Allen Dulles at Supreme Headquarters in Rheims just as the war in the West was ending in 1945. He had arrived on a liaison visit from Berne in Switzerland, where he had been directing the European operations of the United States Office of Strategic Services. The Office of Strategic Services was the cover name for the American secret service which was being organized and developed by Colonel (later General) William J. Donovan, a distinguished lawyer. At that time I was the chief Intelligence officer at General Eisenhower's headquarters and my main knowledge of the Office of Strategic Services came from the confusion that arose from their competition with their British opposite numbers. Many instances of this competitive spirit came to my notice, but I did not consider them important. I felt much sympathy for Donovan and his associates in their task of developing the new United States service and Donovan always expressed to me his gratitude for any help given him, but my main concern, as Eisen-hower's chief Intelligence officer, was to ensure that I had some control over the information they fed to the American staffs under Eisen-hower's command. I possessed this control over information from British sources, and it did not seem to me unreasonable that the Americans should operate in the same way. In fact there was a period when Allen Dulles was responsible for passing a good deal of informa-tion directly to the Americans under Eisenhower—especially informa-tion concerned with the so-called 'National Redoubt' in Germany; if I had not taken steps to counter some of the less reliable information about this 'Redoubt' it could have had a considerable effect on Eisen-hower's strategy.

At this time, Allen Welsh Dulles was fifty-two years of age. The son of a Presbyterian minister and the younger brother of John Foster Dulles, he had graduated from Princeton in 1914. After teaching for eight months at a missionary school in Allahabad in India, he joined the United States foreign service in 1916. He later became involved in the secret peace negotiations with the Austro–Hungarian empire, and also took part in the negotiations which led to the signing of the Treaty of Versailles. He left the American foreign service in 1926 to join the New York legal firm of Sullivan and Cromwell, but when the United States entered World War II his services were once again in demand. He joined the Office of Strategic Services and was appointed to Berne, nominally as assistant to the United States Minister. In fact he was known by everyone in Europe as a special envoy of President Roosevelt, particularly concerned with Intelligence duties. Switzer-land had been a centre for international espionage even before World War I, and it maintained its reputation during World War II in spite of competition from Portugal. As a result, Dulles was besieged by a multitude of informants, many of whom were potentially valuable. Strangely enough, the publicity he received was helpful, for often the difficulty with informants is that they have no idea where to take their information. What Switzerland needed during World War II was a well-known market for intelligence, and this is what Dulles provided.

One of Dulles's most important achievements while he was in Switzerland was to build up a wide network of contacts and spies which eventually brought him in touch with sources of disaffection inside Germany. In May 1944, he received from General Beck, a former German Army Chief of Staff, a detailed plan to end the war, by which the German forces would facilitate the Allied occupation of Germany, while holding the Russians on the Eastern front. This was the last offer of its kind to be received before the Allied invasion of Europe and it was rejected by the British and United States Governments. The contacts which Dulles had developed within Germany also provided him with advance information about the plot to assassinate Hitler on 20 July 1944. At the time I was at Supreme Headquarters, but I do not know whether Eisenhower himself was informed of it; certainly, the Intelligence staffs were not aware or involved. Nevertheless, when I heard of its failure it did surprise me; rather it was the small margin by which it failed that did cause surprise. As a result of my experiences in Berlin before the war I had come to lack faith in the possibility of any widespread or successful conspiracy against Hitler by the German Army. Too many generals had profited by the advent of the Führer and taken the oath of allegiance to him, and adequate leaders for such plots were not available.

When I met Dulles in 1945 he presented me with a gold watch that he had brought from Switzerland, a kind and friendly gesture when watches were almost unobtainable in Britain. My chief memory of him from that time is his infectious, gusty laugh, which always seemed to enter a room with him. Even when I came to know him better in later years I was seldom able to penetrate beyond this laugh, or to conduct any serious professional conversation with him for more than a few sentences. I am sure that this was my fault, but in some ways Dulles always remained an enigma to me, although I never had any doubt that he was a staunch friend to my country.

At the end of the war Dulles returned to his law practice, only to be recalled to government service by President Truman in 1948. The previous year, in September 1947, the National Security Act had come into force and established the Central Intelligence Agency with broad powers and duties. The Act provided that the CIA should report directly to the National Security Council, which advises the President and is chaired by him, and that the functions of the CIA should be: to gather information by covert as well as overt means; to advise the National Security Council on Intelligence matters relating to national security; to make recommendations to the Council for the co-ordination of all governmental Intelligence activities; to correlate and evaluate intelligence and provide for its dissemination within government; to perform for the benefit of existing Intelligence agencies such additional services as the council determines can be efficiently performed centrally; to be prepared to intervene covertly in the affairs of other nations when so directed; and to perform such other functions relating to national security Intelligence as may be directed by the council.

The birth of the new agency in an area in which other military and civilian organizations had vested interests was not without pain, and in 1948 the President asked three New York lawyers, including Dulles, to consider the structure and operations of the Agency, which was then under the direction of Rear Admiral Roscoe Hillenkoetter. Admiral Hillenkoetter had been United States naval attaché in Vichy during World War II, and had rendered very valuable services to the Allied cause.

The report, which was produced in 1949, was critical of some aspects of the Agency's work, and recommended a number of changes, which the National Security Council instructed the Agency to put into effect. For a variety of reasons the implementation of many of these changes waited until the following year, when General Walter Bedell Smith took over the job of Director. He immediately asked Dulles to join him as Deputy Director, and he did so in 1951. In 1953 on Bedell Smith's retirement, Dulles became the first civilian Director of the CIA.

In order to appreciate the importance of this post in the Washington bureaucracy, it is necessary to understand that the head of the CIA wears two hats. First, as Director of the Agency, he is in charge of a massive centralized intelligence machine, responsible for many forms of overt and secret collection activities and for a broad range of collating, evaluating and estimating tasks. In addition, as Director of Central Intelligence, he is charged with the co-ordination of all United States Intelligence activities and operations, and what is more he is by law the chief Intelligence adviser to the President. He attends the National Security Council over which the President presides. In order to perform his co-ordinating role, the Director of Central Intelligence chairs the United States Intelligence Board, the senior committee on Intelligence. The Office of National Estimates, a part of the CIA, which

serves this Board and drafts and co-ordinates the estimates for which
the Board is famous, is responsible to him in his role of Director of
Central Intelligence.

Dulles and his successor, John McCone, were the two Directors of
the CIA with whom I was most closely associated after the war but
I had worked intimately with General Bedell Smith when he was
Eisenhower's Chief of Staff during World War II. Later he served as
American Ambassador in Moscow for nearly three years during the
worst part of the Cold War. With this experience fresh in his mind, and
given his interest in the problems of Military Intelligence, it was not
surprising that he should accept the appointment of Director of the
Agency. He had a curiously ambivalent attitude to the 'secret under-
cover' part of his work. It is my opinion that he never really understood these rather complicated affairs and that it was probably because
he realized this lack within himself that he recruited Allen Dulles as
his deputy. On the other hand, I have always felt that they had some
kind of secret fascination for him; certainly, when enquiries about
the Agency became embarrassing, he tended to use superficial stories of
its secret activities and adventures as a means of diverting the attention
of over-zealous questioners. On one occasion, to my knowledge, he
had taken steps to inform himself of my own actions while I was
Director of the Joint Intelligence Bureau in London. During a call I
paid on him in Washington he produced a thick file and read from it
the record of a conversation I had had with an ex-officer in Germany
some weeks before. Perhaps some parts of this conversation, taken out
of context, could have been regarded as critical of some American
activities. I tried to explain my position, but Bedell Smith made me
account in detail for every statement I was alleged to have made to my
German friend. Finally he closed the file with a bang, and said that was
the end of the matter. I learned my lesson. When in future I felt obliged
to criticize American activities to a third party I was always careful
to make it quite clear that I was prepared to repeat the criticism to the
Americans directly. In spite of his attitude to secret activities, Bedell
Smith did a great deal to improve the organization of the CIA, and to
instill in some of the more refractory members of its staff a sense of
discipline and restraint.

Although I was not surprised when Bedell Smith became Director
of the CIA, I was very surprised when Dulles succeeded him. It had

of course been known for some months that a successor to Bedell Smith was being sought, but, in common with most of the staff of the Agency and the Washington establishment, I had assumed that the new Director would be chosen from outside the ranks of the Agency. The names of many prominent men were in fact being freely mentioned as candidates. My first intimation that Dulles would get the job was a comment from Bedell Smith that in future I might be well advised to treat Allen with a little more deference. Dulles's acceptance of the appointment brought great pleasure to the staff of CIA, as undoubtedly did the appointment of Richard Helms in 1966, for both these men were professional Intelligence officers. Any thoughts that Dulles might devote too much of his energy to his old trade, and become too deeply concerned with intrigue and secret agents, were soon dispelled by events.

Fundamentally, Allen Dulles's views on Intelligence were simple. In the first place, he gave great emphasis to the 'warning' function of the Intelligence machine. He saw the whole world as an area of conflict, in which the prime duty of an Intelligence service was to provide its government with warning of hostile or provocative acts wherever they might occur. He conceded that in international affairs it is often impossible to predict with any precision when or where or why the next crisis will strike, but he firmly believed that a close-knit and coordinated Intelligence community, constantly on the alert, should be able to report accurately and quickly on developments in any part of the globe. He maintained also that men of experience, supported by massive collection operations, could often provide warning of events with sufficient accuracy and in sufficient time for it to be useful to policy and decision-makers. He thought that the fact that warning might well be possible should not be concealed from potential enemies, although the methods and sources by which warning was obtained should be closely guarded. Naturally, he realized that arrangements for what have come to be known as 'current' and 'indications' Intelligence must be supported by equally efficient arrangements for the study of longer-term trends and the preparation of longer-term evaluations, but his greatest interest was in current events and short-term developments.

Dulles was convinced that the collection, collation and analysis of information should be conducted by a central agency of government, which had no responsibility for policy-making and no responsibility for such practical matters as, say, choosing the weapons systems with which United States forces should be armed. He was greatly in favour of the tendency that had become apparent in many countries to amalgamate Military Intelligence services; he believed that useful military estimates could not be prepared in isolation and without regard for economic and social factors. Further, he thought that the most serious occupational hazard for those employed in the Intelligence community was conscious or unconscious bias—the tendency to bend facts to suit preconceived or particular viewpoints or vested interests, and he supported any steps that would help to avoid these dangers.

Dulles was naturally fully aware that many people in the free world were disturbed by certain methods which the United States Intelligence structure felt it necessary to use in so-called peacetime for the collection of information, but, given his earlier Intelligence experience, I doubt if he had many qualms about the development of the more devious methods of collection, such as U2 flights, code-breaking, tunnels from West Berlin for the interception of Soviet and East German telephone communications, covert distribution of funds for the support of Western institutions, and so on. Indeed, his professional enthusiasm was stirred by the more enterprising undertakings. He would have argued that the world was not at peace, and had not been since the communist powers in effect declared war on the West, that the collection of data hurt no one, or very few, and that it was better to collect information which might help to avoid war than merely to prepare for war blindly. Eisenhower fully supported Dulles in these views. The President was firmly convinced that the collection of information about the activities of potential enemies was necessary not only for the defence of the United States, but for the preservation of the non-communist world's freedom. Eisenhower himself reminded me rather sharply of this after the U2 episode.

In many ways the public image of the CIA has suffered because of the clandestine activities of its secret branches, although these are well within the terms of its charter. The Agency, for instance, has been accused of overthrowing the government of Guatemala in 1958, supporting the revolt against President Sukarno of Indonesia in 1958, engineering the Greek coup d'état in 1967, arranging for the capture and death of Che Guevara in 1967 and generally meddling in the internal affairs of foreign states. The two events over which the CIA was most criticized were the shooting down of the U2 reconnaissance aircraft by the Soviet Union on 1 May 1960, two weeks before President Eisenhower was due to meet Khrushchev at a summit meeting in Paris, and the Cuban adventure in April 1961, when the CIA was supposed to have contributed directly to the American disaster in the Bay of Pigs by the provision of inaccurate information.

Neither the U2 incident nor the Bay of Pigs fiasco was necessarily due to errors made by the staff of the CIA. In the case of the U2 it is now known that the affair was largely due to coincidence. For good and sufficient reasons air reconnaissance of the Soviet Union was being conducted as a matter of routine; and as a matter of routine the flights continued in spite of the forthcoming summit meeting. By unfortunate chance, the incident occurred just two weeks before the meeting, so that Khrushchev was able to extract the maximum political advantage from it. Admittedly, some aspects of the United States posture were mishandled—it would probably have been better if the President had not admitted knowledge of the flights—but nevertheless Khrushchev's appearance of injured innocence was very much less than convincing in view of known Soviet espionage operations and activities. Unless Khrushchev had wanted to take advantage of the situation, there was no need for the incident to have affected the summit meeting.

The Bay of Pigs affair was quite different, and there are probably good reasons for suggesting that the whole operation should have been organized by the military authorities in the Pentagon. Admittedly General Lemnitzer, the Chairman of the Joint Chiefs of Staff, and Admiral Arleigh Burke, the Chief of Naval Operations, had both seen the plans and given them their approval, but it is difficult to know how seriously they reviewed the operation and its chances of success. As a result of his experiences with Eisenhower in North Africa, General Lemnitzer tended to look with favour on such quasi-military undertakings, and Admiral Burke was a man to whom almost any action against the communists was a necessity without choice.

I have always assumed that the CIA was covertly involved in the Bay of Pigs operation so that the United States Government could, if it wished, deny any responsibility for the actions of the Cuban exiles. This was surely wishful thinking; no one would ever be convinced that such a military operation could be staged at America's front door unknown to the United States Government and without American co-operation. We now know that the affair was more an operational than an Intelligence failure. President Kennedy's decision to withhold United States air support to the invasion really decided the issue. The CIA was blamed because much of the American press assumed that the operation was conceived on the basis of an ill-founded Intelligence estimate that a landing would lead to a widespread and successful popular revolt in Cuba. Allen Dulles confined himself to one clear statement on the Bay of Pigs episode in his book *The Craft of Intelligence*, and it is only fair to quote him: 'I repeat now what I have said publicly before: I know of no estimate that a spontaneous uprising of the un-armed population of Cuba would be touched off by the landing.'

My experience is that operational and policy errors are often wrongly attributed to inaccurate or insufficient Intelligence. The tactical success of the Germans in the so-called Battle of the Bulge in the Ardennes in the closing stages of World War II was vociferously attributed to the failure of Intelligence staffs to provide warning of German intentions. An inquiry by General Bedell Smith immediately after the war absolved Intelligence of any failure on this occasion; such blame as could be attached to anyone was said to rest with the operational staffs. I think that this discussion of the attribution of blame for failures is a fruitless, though continuing, argument. The remedy lies in bringing Intelligence and operational staff more closely in contact, and I am convinced that Intelligence officers should participate directly in any important planning, policy or operational decision-making, both in war and peace. I have so often been present at meetings of one kind or another at which the boldly expressed 'hunch' or personal convic-tion or 'funny internal feeling' of one individual has all too readily been taken as a considered estimate of a situation. In the absence of an expert whose involvement in the affair is complete, the views of the so-called 'ideas' man are accepted as a guide to action.

Nevertheless, it must be conceded, as Gauché said, that Intelligence estimates can seldom be so complete as to cover every eventuality and possibility. No institution can hope for a completely perfect record, and no Intelligence officer can hope to be right all the time. The most that can be claimed is that where questions of forecasting the capabili-ties and intentions of others are concerned, the centralized Intelligence structure has a greater chance of being right than most other institutions or individual judgements. Especially when the risks are real and the stakes high, it is ridiculous not to listen to its views.

A second feature of Dulles's general attitude to Intelligence is demonstrated by his constant appreciation of the fact that 'customers' for intelligence are made by men, and not created by some act of divine providence. Customers are found by demonstrating an ability to satisfy their explicit or implicit requirements. In business, this is done by means of advertising and salesmanship; Intelligence is one of the few functions of government which must tackle its consumer problems similarly and engage in a constant search for markets. Naturally, the first step is the anticipation of likely consumer needs with a good product. In a sense, the objectives of Intelligence work are to have accurate forecasts of events or stages of development on the desks of decision-makers sufficiently early for them to take action, or, failing this, to have accurate and imaginative estimates of situations on the decision-makers' desks at the same time as the news to which they refer is appearing on the press agency teletype. Obviously, sensible anticipation demands the co-operation of the policy-makers and planners, who must play their part by informing Intelligence staffs of the kinds of matters on which decisions are likely to be made, and the kinds of policies that are being developed.

Dulles also held strong views on the capabilities of his main opponents—the Intelligence service of the Soviet Union. In general, he felt that Soviet Intelligence was over-confident and over-complicated. He believed that the real danger it posed lay not so much in individual exploits of Soviet spies as in the magnitude of its efforts, the money available, the immense number of persons it employed, the lengths to which the Soviet authorities were prepared to go to achieve their purposes and the losses they were willing to sustain in the process. He thought that a ruthless structure of this magnitude could hardly fail to achieve a broad measure of success.

Personally, I would differ with Dulles on this point. I have considerable doubts about the value of the Soviet 'end-product'—the documents and appreciations which result from the efforts at collection and the processes of collation, evaluation and estimating. Undoubtedly the Soviet Intelligence community receives a massive volume of information, and this volume is likely to continue to grow. Ultimately, in spite of whatever efforts are made to automate the processing of this information, the end-product must rely on the exercise of human judgement. And judgement depends on the experience of the judge. In other words, I have some doubts whether the Soviet community has sufficient numbers of persons with adequate and objective knowledge of foreign countries to make the best use of the information or assessments it receives. There is also little doubt that the Soviet community suffers to a marked degree from the incubus of doctrinaire doctoring of reports which are selectively biased by the reporter and read in a wishful way by the recipient.

Three major Soviet Intelligence failures will help to demonstrate this point about defective understanding of the outside world. First, the decision to deploy offensive surface-to-surface missiles in Cuba, aimed at the United States, showed a lamentable misunderstanding of the American mind and likely American responses. Possibly this was a personal decision of Khrushchev based on his experiences at the meeting with Kennedy in Vienna in 1961, when it may well have seemed to him that he was in a position of psychological and material superiority over the young President. The Soviet decision was clearly based on a gamble that a *fait accompli* could be achieved in the guise of defensive aid to Cuba. Soviet Intelligence apparently failed to estimate correctly the probable strength of the United States response to such an operation ninety miles from the Florida coast.

A second failure was shown by the events in the Middle East in 1967. It is generally accepted that the Soviet authorities encouraged the Arab States to throw down the gauntlet to the Israelis. Presumably they would not have done this unless their Intelligence estimators had assured them that the Arab States with their liberal supplies of Soviet equipment were likely to win, or at least not likely to be defeated so decisively by a pre-emptive attack. The decision concerning the attitude to be adopted towards Arab military aspirations was classic, in the sense that it could not reasonably have been taken without an Intelligence input. This input was obviously wrong, both in terms of warning, for apparently it failed to warn of the likelihood of an Israeli attack, and in terms of estimates of capabilities, for presumably it wildly underestimated the Israelis' strength, operational efficiency and determination.

Thirdly, I believe that Soviet Intelligence completely failed to understand the repercussions that would follow the occupation of

Czechoslovakia by Soviet troops in 1968. Possibly in view of the Soviet leadership there were overriding reasons why this action would have been taken even if an adequate Intelligence estimate had been available, such as the need to seal off and control a critically weak key sector in Central Europe, but Soviet attitudes during and after the invasion would appear to me to indicate that the reactions of the Czech people and the international reactions were both unexpected.

In short I incline to the belief that the Soviet Intelligence organization, in spite of its enormous resources and the vast efforts it makes to acquire information, is a captive of its environment and its traditions and may not be able to sort the wheat from the chaff, and present the Soviet decision-makers with accurate and timely information. What is more, I see serious dangers in this unbalanced situation where Soviet Intelligence is of poor quality, while the United States authorities have access to a sophisticated and high quality product. The dangers lie in the fact that the United States leaders may assume that their Russian opposite numbers are as fully aware of the facts and implications of a given situation (such as, for example, the 1967 Middle East crisis) as they themselves are, and that Soviet responses to United States moves will be based on a common understanding, when this is not in fact the case. Steps to avoid this have of course been taken—the so-called 'hot line' between Washington and Moscow is an example. Further, it is true that more conceptual matters, about, say, the strategic balance, are largely dealt with in open literature, and current thinking on such matters can be freely read by both sides. Nevertheless, I am not sure that if I were attempting to bring about or improve a state of détente between East and West, I should not recommend an effort by Intelligence staffs on both sides to agree on data, perhaps in the first place about countries other than themselves and finally on their own respective capabilities. It seems to me that the mutual understanding that would arise from such a process would contribute a great deal to the normalization of relations. I suppose that the idea of 'pooling' Intelligence data and estimates between East and West will seem horrifying to many Intelligence officers. Perhaps all I am saying, somewhat metaphorically, is that if the peace of the world is to rest on the actions and reactions of the two super-powers, it would be as well if the two powers were to agree on the kind of world with which they were dealing and the range of actions and responses that lie within their capabilities. Even an agreement as to the limits within which competition between them should be carried on might be of value.

Allen Dulles was undoubtedly the greatest United States professional Intelligence officer of his time, although he was perhaps stronger and more interested in matters concerned with collection and short-term evaluation than in the business of long-range estimating. He was not unaware of his unique experience. In spite of the slightly bantering attitude with which he approached serious matters, there was a certain hardness in his character, and he knew that his position effectively made him the doyen of the free world's Intelligence activity. Competitors were not entirely welcome, and he had an active dislike of being associated with a failure. Nevertheless, he was generous in praise of others, and a great friend to Britain. I remember that when I was in Washington just after Eisenhower's election in December 1952, Dulles invited me to his home to meet his brother John Foster Dulles, who was about to become Eisenhower's Secretary of State. The object of the occasion was to make known to John Foster Dulles the close relationship that I had maintained with the United States Intelligence community, and to express the hope that this relationship would continue under the Republican administration. All happened as Allen had planned; John Foster said immediately and without hesitation that there would be no interruption of our contacts. The ending of the visit was sad. The telephone rang, and Allen was told about the serious condition of his only son, who had been wounded in Korea.

I suppose that history must judge the extent to which Allen Dulles's reputation was justified. In some ways he was the last of the great Intelligence officers whose stock-in-trade consisted of secrets and mysteries. He might without disrespect be described as the last great Romantic of Intelligence. Almost certainly if he had remained longer as Director of the CIA his attitudes would have changed, because with the advent of the Kennedy regime the Intelligence director was to become less a man of mysteries and more a participant in affairs and decisions. There is no reason to suppose that such a change would have been unacceptable to Dulles, for in spite of his early preoccupations with intrigue, he had a basic urge to ensure that the end-product of the Intelligence process was used.

After the Bay of Pigs episode, Dulles offered his resignation to the new President, but it was not immediately accepted for this would have made him the unjustified scapegoat for the failure of the enterprise. Nevertheless there was a general consensus in the new administration that a change should be made, and a search for a successor was commenced. It was, however, very difficult if not impossible to find candidates with qualifications, experience or knowledge that approached those of Dulles. In the end the choice fell on John A. McCone, a successful business man who had made a fortune in shipping and engineering, and had then undertaken a most successful second career in government service.

Dulles retired in September 1961. The last years of his life seemed to me rather sad; perhaps he found it difficult to adjust to the change from being at the centre of affairs to living in his deserted house in Q Street in Washington. Certainly he still had his friends and his contacts, but he was no longer eagerly sought out as a source of information. He served on the Commission that enquired into the circumstances surrounding the assassination of President Kennedy, but in the main he watched the world from the sidelines. He died in 1969.

*

John A. McCone took control of the CIA in September 1961, at the age of 59. He had been a distinguished president and chief executive of a number of large corporations, and had served the United States Government between 1948 and 1951 as a Deputy to the Secretary of Defense and Under Secretary of the United States Air Force, and in 1958 he was asked to become Chairman of the United States Atomic Energy Commission. In this post he studied Soviet nuclear developments, and became interested in the Russian scene and Russian character. While the quest for a successor to Dulles was in progress, McCone had a chance interview with President Kennedy at which the subject of Soviet achievements was raised. The insight which McCone displayed convinced the President that here was the ideal new Director for the CIA. McCone accepted the appointment, although at the time the position must have appeared to have few attractions, for the Bay of Pigs affair had shown how readily a reputation could be sacrificed in this complex and demanding field. I remember commenting at a dinner given for me by McCone soon after he took over that he must be prepared to be the subject of continuous public criticism, and that he would rarely be able to reply in kind or publicly to justify his actions.

Most of the Washington establishment and the senior officers of the CIA thought that because of his business background McCone would concentrate on the management of the Agency, and leave substantive Intelligence questions to others. In fact, Dulles had already solved most of the administrative problems which had beset the Agency; even the new headquarters outside Washington was nearly completed (it was opened by President Kennedy at the end of November 1961). McCone quickly became absorbed in Intelligence, and rapidly acquired a considerable expertise in the field, which the professionals of CIA came to respect. His range of technical knowledge and his experience in business and government enabled him to grasp readily the more sophisticated problems associated with assessments of longer-term strategic, economic and technological threats or competition. He did this in a way which Allen Dulles, with his major interest in collection and his less technical approach, might not have managed.

In a sense Allen Dulles and John McCone represent two eras. The former can be seen mainly in the terms of the great Intelligence espionage 'coup'. The latter was wedded to that part of the Intelligence process concerned with evaluation—the forming of judgements on the basis of an insight that comprehends technical and scientific, as well as political, strategic and military factors. McCone, with his white hair, his pinkish complexion and his penetrating gaze through glinting spectacles, sometimes seemed to have a little of the clinician about him. Quiet, calm, courteous and with ready smile, he could easily be seen as a diagnostician at a large teaching hospital. He gave an impression of great strength, firm judgement and steely purpose, and his manner formed a considerable contrast to that of Allen Dulles.

McCone's newly-acquired expertise was very soon to be tested in one of the most difficult situations ever faced by an Intelligence authority—the Cuban missile crisis of October 1962. Early in that year, President Kennedy had extended the United States commitment to Vietnam, reorganized the so-called Alliance for Progress, and responded to communist pressures in Berlin, South-East Asia and Latin America. During the summer, official Washington was aware of rumours that the Soviet Union intended to position long-range missiles in Cuba, but the general view was that there would be no attempt to install a major offensive capability, and most people agreed that the Soviet authorities were building surface-to-air missile sites with which to defend Cuba against the air attacks that would accompany an attempt at invasion. McCone's own reasoning was a good deal more sophisticated than this. He thought that the surface-to-air missiles would be useless against an invasion force because they could not destroy aircraft at altitudes of less than 10,000 feet, and would in any case quickly succumb to a determined attack. He believed that the real reason for the deployment of the anti-aircraft missiles was to prevent aerial surveillance, and thus conceal any further military deployments that might be taking place on the island. Further, he argued, only an attempt to install long-range surface-to-surface missiles could justify such extreme efforts at concealment.

McCone was so convinced of the truth of his theory that even while on his honeymoon in Florida—he had married for the second time in August—he continued to urge his deputy to press these views on the President. All Intelligence sources were exploited in an effort to prove or disprove the theory, but it was not until 14 October that an air force officer flew the reconnaissance mission which was to have such dramatic results. The photographs which resulted from the sortie demonstrated that McCone was right. Some members of the Washington community described McCone's far-sighted logic as a chance 'hunch', but I think his views resulted from his understanding of the Soviet mind, his ability to study his staff's analyses, but nevertheless to remain sceptical of 'conventional wisdom', and a certain steadfastness of purpose which enabled him to continue to press his views at a time when many of his colleagues regarded them as unsupported opinions.

The contribution which McCone's shrewd judgement made to the national decision process during the thirteen days of the Cuban missile crisis has been insufficiently acknowledged. In general, it was McCone's judgement that the Soviet leaders would not react violently in Berlin or elsewhere to any non-violent measures contemplated by the United States. This view encouraged the President and the so-called 'Executive Committee', which guided America's destiny through those dark days, to decide on the option of blockade—an option which was later to be proved successful. The Executive Committee with the President in the chair regularly opened its proceedings with a briefing by McCone—a daily ritual which has been described as of overpowering solemnity. Nevertheless, at a time when few were acting in character, when the bold tended to be timid and the timid bold, the presence of a McCone, cool, calculating, far-seeing and with the facts at his finger-tips, was invaluable.

More generally, McCone had a particular attribute which I con-sider vital for any Intelligence officer in a senior position; this is a desire—preferably fanatical—to ensure that decisions are based on such Intelligence as is available. McCone visited South Vietnam in March 1964 with Robert S. McNamara, the Secretary of Defense. His report on the visit suggested a far less optimistic picture of the situation in that area than did his colleague's. The President was thus faced with differing estimates of the situation, and different policy recommenda-tions. The differences could not be bridged, so McCone, realizing that his first responsibility was to present the Intelligence information and not to make policy, withdrew his policy recommendations, but insisted that his Intelligence estimate should remain on the record unchanged as his input to the solution of the problems.* From this occasion there developed a somewhat wasteful competition between the CIA and the Pentagon to be the first to provide the President with a new piece of information or intelligence. A good deal of effort was expended by both the CIA and the Pentagon's Defense Intelligence Agency (a new inter-service organization which had been established in 1961 to supply the Secretary of Defense with Military Intelligence uncoloured by single-service implications) in efforts to 'scoop' the other and elaborate procedures were developed in the hope of winning the race to the President by even a few seconds. In some senses this rivalry was useful, especially in times of crisis, but one of its less helpful aspects was the temptation it engendered to use relatively trivial in-formation as a basis for dramatic speculation.

As far as McCone was concerned, his determination to be first with any data was based on two principles: it was his responsibility as Direc-tor of Central Intelligence to inform the President on all Intelligence matters; and he distrusted estimates prepared by military officers. Eisenhower had come to have little faith in military thinking and to be sceptical of estimates prepared by the so-called 'military-industrial' complex in the United States. McCone was close to the ex-President,

---

* See Weintal and Bartlett: *Facing the Brink.*

and it is possible that he acquired his scepticism about military thinking from Eisenhower. Certainly he made no secret of his views. I remember that on one occasion he enquired bluntly if British Intelligence estimates were the responsibility of a serviceman or a civilian. He was assured that the Chairman of the Joint Intelligence Committee was a civilian, and appeared to be reassured.

McCone's attitude to policy-making has been of the greatest significance to United States Intelligence. The relationship between Intelligence officers and policy-makers is of course difficult and complex. The generally accepted view that it is the duty of the Intelligence officer to 'give just the facts, please' has little relevance in a modern governmental structure. In the first place, the facts are often such that the policy-makers are unable to interpret them without expert advice. Secondly, and obviously, the choice of facts is critical, and the Intelligence officer's decision as to which facts are relevant and which should be presented to the policy-makers is often the major initial step in the decision process. This choice between the trivial and the sensational, between the unpleasant and the pleasing, is by no means as easy as it may appear. Intelligence officers are human, too, and the temptations to prepare a logical story or to serve personal prejudices cannot be overlooked, especially in areas where the facts themselves are often in some doubt and the interpretation of them is as much a matter of opinion as of logic.

On the other hand, there is a frequent temptation for policy-makers to use Intelligence data selectively to suit their own preconceived judgements or political requirements. McCone's great virtue was that he saw all sides of these questions, and was sufficiently broad-minded to appreciate that they had no simple answers. In particular, although his grasp of affairs was such that he could readily assume the role of competent and well-informed critic of policy, he nevertheless accepted the limitations inherent in his role as chief Intelligence officer, but without de-emphasizing the constructive contributions which Intelligence must make to the decision process. He remained very conscious of the constant need to be in the closest touch with the key members of the United States Government, the President and some half-dozen others. He regarded it as his personal responsibility to see that the quintessential end-product of the huge United States Intelligence apparatus was effectively registering at the top.

McCone left the CIA in April 1965, and his chair was occupied for some fourteen months by Admiral W. F. Raborn. After that, in June 1966, Richard Helms, a professional like Dulles, was appointed to the post, a position which he continues to hold.

The three Directors of the CIA that I have known best—Bedell Smith, Dulles and McCone—all came to the appointment when they were already well known in American official and public life. All three, because of their records, were able to command attention in Washington. None of them was prepared to assemble facts and figures quietly and then sit passively by while someone else placed unwarranted interpretations on the data they had supplied. Cavendish-Bentinck had a great deal in common with Dulles and McCone. None was a military expert in the ordinary sense, and McCone probably had the best grasp of military matters at the higher levels. Cavendish-Bentinck and Dulles had somewhat similar diplomatic backgrounds, but I reiterate that the characteristic that all three of these men shared was a broad and informed understanding of the world of affairs and of the curious combinations of pressures in the light of which great decisions are reached. As well as being about foreign countries Intelligence is, like diplomacy, fundamentally about people and their concerns and decisions and reactions. Possibly the reactions of those concerned are only seen in terms of hardware or events—a new missile, a new formation, a new offensive, a new political initiative—but the sort of experience that is needed at the highest levels of Intelligence, and which enables one to discount pseudo-happenings and to pass behind events to an understanding of motivations and intentions, is hard to come by. Both Britain and the United States have been fortunate to have had the services of these men of Intelligence.

6

SPIES

I have always had doubts about the usefulness of secret services and secret agents, especially in the military field, and more especially when the results of their efforts are considered in the broad context of all Intelligence sources and operations. I tend to agree with the comment of Admiral Wemyss, the British First Sea Lord at the end of World War I, that the product of secret Intelligence is 'uncertain information from questionable people'.

These opinions are strengthened by the stories of the men of Intelligence we have examined in this book. Spies failed Nicolai and Hentsch in the critical days of September 1914. Haig received little information from secret services about the internal affairs of Germany. Some information of this kind was available to Gauché in the years between the wars, but no spy provided precise details of Hitler's coups, nor of the German attack in 1940. The Germans had extraordinarily little knowledge of the movements of the British Expeditionary Force in World War I, and no spies told them about radar, or when and where Eisenhower would land in 1944.

Nevertheless I do not want to overstate the case. It is only in the popular imagination that spies and spying have come to represent the whole of Intelligence. In practice, reports from spies are merely one of the contributions to the total Intelligence picture, and perhaps their chief value is to add to the mass of items of varying precision and varying reliability through which the Intelligence analyst must sift. While he is sifting, the analyst must always remember that an agent's stock-in-trade is the production of information, and that he is constantly under pressure to justify his existence by the transmission of something to his superior. What is more, it is naturally a characteristic of agents and those handling them to believe that their information is not only accurate, but also of exceptional and exclusive value. Analysts who have at their disposal material from a wide variety of sources tend to be less enthusiastic.

Whenever a spy is arrested and tried I read of the immense value to those who employed him of the information he has passed, but I sometimes wonder whether their opponents find this to be so. The first problem is to guarantee its authenticity, and this can often be very difficult. History is full of examples of the downright 'plant'—the marked map which is intended to deceive, the body with false information in its pockets that is 'drowned' near an enemy shore. It seems to me that more often than not the possibility of deception is sufficient to deter the recipient from making effective use of information. There have been some occasions when both true or false information has been used by one side or the other in a conflict, but I suspect there are many more occasions when authentic documents were discarded as of doubtful reliability.

Agents' reports quite often turn out to be rehashes of information that has already appeared in the press or other published sources. I remember that during World War II I sometimes received in the form of agents' reports estimates or parts of estimates that I or my staff had prepared. This did not surprise me. These estimates were often given wide distribution to many persons who in wartime conditions could not be fully 'screened', and must eventually have found their way into the hands of those who felt they could profit from them. There is a thriving market for any reports—especially 'Intelligence' reports—which bear any kind of stamp of authenticity; their value is heightened if the paper on which they are printed bears the legend, 'This document is the property of the Government of . . .', or if they carry well-known signatures. I have sometimes wondered whether the market for counterfeit official documents has been adequately exploited by those who are accustomed to drafting in 'officialese'.

At least one such attempt at exploitation took place in Germany in 1922, and became known as the Anspach case. Anspach was a German communist who was arrested by the police. When his house was searched there was discovered a treasure trove of impressive documents on such subjects as the organization of the German military police and German mobilization plans, together seemingly with secret cabinet papers. The police were aghast; apparently they had in their hands a master spy. Wide publicity resulted, and the German Government ordered the closest examination of the documents. It was eventually found that the information about the military police consisted of names taken wholesale from a Berlin directory, and the secret cabinet papers were made up from newspaper reports and records of debates in the Reichstag. The whole lot were forgeries. Anspach was quietly sent to a lunatic asylum.

Occasionally spies do appear in positions in which they can obtain information of an apparently crucial nature; usually, however, such an operation requires the recruitment or placement of an agent in the top echelons of another nation's bureaucratic hierachy, and this is difficult without years of preparatory effort, to which only a few governments are prepared to devote the necessary time and resources. The government of the Soviet Union is one of these, and the Russians seem able to achieve successes in the field of espionage that on the whole elude the Western world. Possibly one of the reasons for their success lies in those national characteristics that have led to the supremacy of the Russian novel—an innate understanding of psychology and a flair for detecting personal motivations.

Even in the best of circumstances the value of information from spies is often limited, at least in terms of the use made of it. During his campaigns Marlborough was on occasions supplied with the complete plans of his French opponents, which had been stolen by a highly placed spy in Paris. There seems little doubt that these plans were authentic, but Marlborough regarded them as mere confirmation of what he already knew or estimated. In other words, the commander preferred his own information and his own judgement to the best that secret sources could provide. In 1862, while the British Admiralty was still wedded to its traditional 'Hearts of Oak', the French sent their first ironclad warship, the *Normandie*, on a voyage across the Atlantic. The French authorities, aware that their ship represented a great advance in naval technology, were naturally anxious to keep secret the details of the voyage. However, the British circumvented French precautions and managed to transmit to Whitehall a copy of the Captain's report on the voyage, with the special request that the document be kept secret so as not to endanger special sources of information. Clearly this was a case where a spy had obtained valuable and reliable information. It would be pleasant to report that the information had an immediate effect on the Admiralty's attitude to the new technology, but I am not sure that this was so.

During World War II, the valet to the British Ambassador in Ankara, who operated under the cover-name 'Cicero', was in the habit of extracting documents from his master's safe and selling them to the Germans. These papers are said to have been of extreme secrecy, and to have revealed many of the operational plans of the Allies. Owing to internal jealousies between rival Intelligence organizations in Germany, however, the Germans failed to make use of the information. They paid Cicero in counterfeit sterling notes, and he vainly attempted to obtain compensation from the post-war West German Government for his valuable, though unused, information.

The Germans claim that during their campaign against Russia in World War II they managed to recruit a renegade Russian commissar into their service and install him in the Kremlin, whence he forwarded important information on Soviet military affairs to them. However well authenticated communications of this kind appear to be, they are bound to come under suspicion as 'plants' designed to mislead the recipients, and there is evidence of at least one case in which the Germans did not accept as accurate information that they received from their source in the Kremlin.

Unless an agent has the luck or ingenuity to lay his hands on a genuine secret document, reporting on political matters is more often than not an expression of the agent's personal opinion. If the source can be identified, and his competence as an observer judged by the user, this information may be useful. Usually, however, security rules do not permit any realistic contact between users and sources and the identities of the latter remain wrapped in mystery. Although they are often claimed to be 'reliable', their veracity can only be checked by reference to the past experience of the service operating the source. Clearly, this complication makes judgement difficult; it would be unusual for an analyst or estimator to regard the unsupported views of an unknown character as more likely to be accurate than his own.

In this context it is of some interest to compare information obtained by secret methods with that obtained from other, perhaps surer, better and less costly, sources. I realize that the following incidents represent only a random sample of stories, and cannot be used to prove my thesis; nevertheless, they at least indicate the nature of the point at issue.

Captain Stehlin of the French Air Force was actively concerned with an Italian military delegation which visited Paris in 1935 to discuss with the French authorities military plans in the event of war with Germany. During the visit Stehlin became very friendly with the general in charge of the Italian delegation. A year later, Stehlin was an assistant air attaché at the French Embassy in Berlin. One day in April 1936, on his way to lunch at the Air Force Club with a senior German officer,

General von Bülow, Stehlin happened to call at the bar of the Hotel Eden, at that time a well-known rendezvous for international visitors. To his surprise he saw in the bar his Italian friend, surrounded by almost the identical group of officers that had been with him in Paris a year before co-ordinating French and Italian war plans. All were in civilian clothes. Stehlin went across and greeted the group, and expressed his surprise at seeing them in Berlin, but it was at once clear that his questions about the reasons for their visit were unwelcome to the Italians. Moreover, Stehlin recognized amongst the German officers present a certain Major von Donat, head of the German Air Intelligence section whose particular task it was to study the French Air Force, and who was incidentally due to join him at lunch with General von Bülow.

Stehlin saw almost immediately that he had stumbled upon an incident of potentially great interest, and his suspicions were further aroused when at lunch General von Bülow made an obviously spurious excuse for the absence of von Donat. Lunch over, Stehlin returned to the Hotel Eden and, using the pretext of personal acquaintanceship, tried to discover where he could contact his Italian friends. He found that the receptionists were unco-operative; they professed complete ignorance of the Italian visitors, and refused to accept a message for them.

Stehlin reported the incident to his ambassador, André François-Poncet, who immediately sent to Paris an account of this highly significant indication of German-Italian military collaboration, commenting that he had received reports from other sources, and notably from the Italian Embassy itself, which tended to confirm the fact of this collaboration. If information of this kind had been received from a secret agent it is doubtful if full credence would have been given to it. The agent's powers of observation would have been questioned, and his ability to identify either von Donat or the Italian general would have been doubted. But coming from a trained, competent and trusted observer who was known to understand the previous history of the Italian group, it was of outstanding value as one of the earliest indications that Germany and Italy had agreed upon joint arrangements for military planning.

In the early 1930s the Deuxième Bureau was concerned about the strength and nature of Italian defences in Libya. The picture they had been able to put together on the basis of reports from agents was fragmentary and clearly inaccurate. The true position was finally ascertained by a French officer, later General Beaufre, who managed to obtain permission to visit the area, and incidentally did so at his own expense. He brought back undeniable proof that the Italians were maintaining double the number of divisions that the Deuxième Bureau had suspected. It is perhaps of incidental interest that the Mareth defence line, which was one of the obstacles facing Montgomery's Eighth Army at the end of its advance through the Western Desert in World War II, had originally been erected by the French against the possibility of an Italian attack from Libya.

In his book *The Congress of Vienna*, Harold Nicolson comments on the espionage activities of the Austrian secret police while the Congress was in progress in 1814 and 1815. The situation has a familiar ring. Apparently the agents who supplied information to the police about the activities of the delegates ranged from men and women of the world who moved on the fringes of society, to housemaids who emptied the waste-paper baskets of the less careful delegates. Personally, I have little doubt that the 'well-placed government official' who undoubtedly figured as the source of many of the police reports was often the hall porter at the Imperial Ministry. As Nicolson says, the ineptitude of the reports was inconceivable. 'The King of Prussia', it was solemnly reported, 'this morning visited the Archduke Charles. In the evening he went out in civilian clothes with a round hat pulled down over his eyes. He had not returned at 10 p.m. The Emperor of Russia went out at 7 p.m. with one of his aides-de-camp. It is believed he went to visit the Princess Thurn and Taxis. Every morning a large block of ice is brought to the Emperor with which he washes his face and hands.' Such reports were not particularly helpful or harmful; neither were they especially entertaining. Even details of the sexual adventures of the less exhausted delegates would have been preferable and certainly more readable. But some of the reports collected by the Austrian police did create damaging suspicions and led to immense mistrust amongst the delegates. As Nicolson says, 'No one can study the reports provided . . . during the Congress of Vienna without realizing the dangerous futility of the whole [espionage] system.'

I am not altogether sure that things have improved a great deal in the last century and a half. Agents' reports still tend to achieve importance not because of their contents, but because of the ingenuity with which the information in them has been obtained, and the personal risks which have often been run by the agent concerned. There remain many who avidly devour agents' reports; such persons are usually those who do not have to make use of the information they contain. In many ways the more trivial the detail, the greater the attractions of these reports. Before World War II the domestic and sex lives of foreign ministers, the aberrations of generals and the pecuniary ambitions of politicians had wide circulation and found appreciative readers. No detail was too small or too unimportant to be reported. A tender letter to a potentate visiting our shores from a mistress whom he had left behind, inquiring amongst other things whether he was being forced to eat 'porridge' every morning, was considered either to be a cunning code or to have some exotic meaning which might reveal a character weakness that could be exploited.

One of the most important pieces of information of all time was of a nature that would not have been believed if it had appeared in an agent's report. This was the news of the Soviet explosion of their first nuclear device. In 1947 most United States experts believed that the early construction of an atomic weapon was well beyond Russian scientific and industrial capabilities. Those who thought that the Soviet Union might test a device in five years' time—by 1952—were considered to be alarmist; the majority of those competent to pass judgement on the issue were virtually certain that the first test would not take place for many years. In spite of these comforting assurances Admiral Lewis Strauss, then Chairman of the United States Atomic Energy Commission, became convinced that the United States should develop special equipment and establish a monitoring system to detect the results of any nuclear explosion from the analysis of air samples. His anxiety proved to be fully justified, for in September 1949 President Truman was able to announce to the world that one of the aircraft operating as part of this detection system had returned with air samples which proved beyond doubt that a nuclear explosion had occurred in Russia. No agent would have been likely to obtain this information, and even if one had been lucky or ingenious enough I think it highly unlikely that the United States authorities would have given his information any credence in the face of the opinions of their own experts.

I do not claim that spies are entirely useless; I merely have doubts concerning the real benefits that are gained from the large costs and risks that their employment involves, and the true usefulness of much of the information from untested, or less reliable, or third- or fourth-hand sources. Nevertheless, there are many occasions when agents produce information which is of value when considered in conjunction with other sources. While Allen Dulles was in charge of the operations of the Office of Strategic Services in Switzerland during World War II he made contact through an intermediary with a well-placed source in Berlin. The intricate arrangements which Dulles devised for contacting and communicating with the agent and the ingenious methods by which his identity was protected have become of classic significance in the field of clandestine Intelligence. The agent produced a lengthy series of reports containing information about German morale in the face of Allied bombing, German plans to combat the French resistance movement, the smuggling of tungsten through Spain to Germany in an effort to evade the Allied blockade, German industrial production, and, later, the conspiracy against Hitler which reached a climax in the abortive attempt on the Führer's life in July 1944.

All this information was naturally of considerable interest, but on the whole it had little value except in the most general context. It can, I think, be reasonably argued that the direct effect of the information on the conduct or outcome of the war may not have been such as to justify the great risks and costs which attended its collection. Nevertheless I concede that one cannot know in advance what information a well-placed source is likely to obtain or what the ultimate significance of the information he obtains is likely to be. For instance, although I was convinced at the time that the so-called conspiracy against Hitler would have only a marginal effect on the course of the war. it might have been of considerable importance; if it had been the beginning of a serious and popular uprising against the Nazi regime and thus demanded decisions concerning, say, the supply of arms to insurgents inside Germany, our knowledge of its details might well have been beyond value.

Spies can provide confirmation of reports from other sources; occasionally they can give an early indication that something unusual may be taking place, that a certain policy is being considered by this or that government. In particular they can perform these functions if the information relates to a physical presence or establishment and is thus susceptible of being checked on the ground. Agents' reports did in fact play important parts in the masses of information which were assembled to solve two of the major Intelligence problems of the later years of the war: the location of the factories which produced two new German aircraft—the Me 262 and the Me 163— which started to appear in combat in the spring of 1943, and the identification during 1943 and 1944 of the German rocket research and development establishment at Peenemunde, and the launching sites for V1 and V2 rockets. The stories of these Intelligence operations are lengthy and complicated and have been told elsewhere. Sometimes agents provided the first hints of areas which might be rewarding targets for aerial reconnaissance sorties, while on other occasions they were asked to examine on the ground areas which appeared from photographs to be suspicious.

In spite of the costs and risks of secret services, most governments maintain them in one form or another. Sometimes, as in the United States, they form part of a central agency which is also responsible for collation, evaluation and estimating; sometimes they operate as a separate department or independent agency, as in Britain today; occasionally, as in pre-war Germany, two or more establishments operate competing systems of agents. The Soviet authorities have always appeared to place great reliance on espionage operations, and the activities of their agents is evidenced by a long succession of notorious cases, from Abel and Fuchs to Blake and Lonsdale.

Some smaller countries with clearly-defined opponents have apparently been able to employ agents with some success. The case of Elie Cohen, an Israeli who managed to gain access to high-level political and military circles in Syria, demonstrates this point. He was eventually traced because the radio which he used to communicate with Tel Aviv interfered with other traffic, but before his arrest he is alleged to have provided information which was vital to the success of Israeli operations against Syria in the Six Day War of 1967. Without access to Israeli records it is hard to judge the extent to which this claim can be justified, but I think that within the relatively limited frame of reference represented by the Arab–Israeli confrontation a spy could well have achieved a major coup.

Clearly all governments must take measures to deal with the threats posed by espionage activities, even if the end-products of the operations are only occasionally of real importance. Possibly the most difficult problem is posed by the true double-agent, who is in touch with two or more Intelligence services, and is operating for each against the other. Colonel Redl, whom I have already mentioned, was one such double-agent, and there have been a number of other examples recently. Some years ago the Hollywood film director Boris Morros was paid by Soviet contacts to recruit American intellectuals and scientists who might have access to classified information. Morros informed the FBI of the situation, and the United States authorities maintained contact with him during the period of his employment by the Russians. Finally, at an appropriate moment, the FBI was able to arrest many who had been prepared to enter the Soviet network.

As I have indicated, there is no doubt whatsoever that a great deal of espionage or attempted espionage is carried on in the modern world. What is more difficult to ascertain is the extent to which nations profit from the information they obtain by these means. My view is that agents generally rank low in the hierarchy of useful sources. Of the mass of information which today floods an Intelligence agency, perhaps five per cent comes from agents' reports; some 30 per cent results from the observations and conversations of attachés and diplomats, while most of the remainder arises from the examination of the press and published material of all kinds and from radio broadcasts. A small but growing percentage comes from other more technical sources. Sources, however, are indivisible, and it is the final picture which emerges from the study of all the information that is of ultimate importance; in this final picture the spy's contribution will be found to be marginal. The spy may remain the hero of the fiction writer and the television screen, but the true men of Intelligence will remain amongst those who devote their attention to the collation and evaluation of information from many different sources, and who form a critical judgement on which military operations, political policy, and business decisions can be based.

7

WHAT IS INTELLIGENCE?

The Intelligence process is neither complex nor obscure. It is based on two premises: that sensible policies can be developed and sensible decisions made only when the facts of the case are known; and that warning concerning decisions that must be made in the nearer or distant future is useful. Just as a television receiver searches for and accepts raw signals from outside itself, transforming these signals into an intelligible and useful picture, so the Intelligence machine collects, collates and evaluates information, and interprets it to provide both 'facts' and 'forecasts'. Clearly the facts must sometimes be less than factual; often they can be little more than expert guesses. Similarly forecasts can only very occasionally be firm prophecies; usually they are only informed and considered estimates, representing a framework within which different courses may be followed. Nevertheless, in spite of these limitations, the organized attempt to assemble 'facts' and prepare 'forecasts' must be regarded as one of the most important activities of government.

There are, as I have indicated, a wide variety of sources upon which an Intelligence community can draw; most of these sources are overt, some covert; some involve no more than reading newspapers and periodicals, while others involve the most expensive and complex technology. Usually there are few risks attached to the acquisition of information, but occasionally important data are only acquired at the cost of a life. Peacetime and wartime sources are rather different, for once contact with an enemy has been established captured documents and the interrogation of prisoners provide a great deal of the most useful information. The equivalent in peacetime is the occasional defector, some of whom have been of great importance.

Once the information has been acquired, it must be collated, evaluated and interpreted. These processes are those which demand the most highly qualified staff, and the greatest rigour. In general terms the work is not unlike that undertaken by any scholar, and the basic processes are 'reading, thinking and writing'. There is, however, one major difference between academic and Intelligence life: a mistake in the academic field may perhaps expose one to the laughter of one's fellows, although it sometimes seems to me that academic communities and conferences are carefully designed to avoid precisely this eventuality, while mistakes in the real world of government may have incalculable effects upon the policy- and decision-making of the nation or even its survival.

The problems that arise in the area of evaluation and interpretation are largely concerned with the provision of adequate means for the assimilation of the mass of information that modern sources and means of communication make available, and with the distinctions between current Intelligence and long-term estimates. The modern analyst can readily be overwhelmed with material, and it must always be remembered that if an adequate end-product is to be provided, all the available data on a given subject must at some point be assembled in one place and in one mind. This is what Gauché and the Deuxième Bureau learned and found so essential and where the Germans made their greatest mistake about priorities for Intelligence. This one mind may well have the support of large staffs who will summarize reports and provide some guidance as to their apparent relative importance, and undoubtedly the product of this mind will be subject to review and vetting by superiors and committees; but in many senses the vital link in the chain of events that results in the Intelligence end-product is the mind of the man who 'reads, thinks and writes'. Recent advances in data processing technology make it clear that computers can assist with the processing of this mass of material, but there seems to me no possibility that a computer can replace the skill and judgement of the Intelligence estimator. The criteria for judging the relevance and importance of given items of intelligence are stored in the experience of the Intelligence officer.

The allocation of resources between so-called 'current Intelligence' which is concerned with the immediate and the short term, and longer-term estimating or forecasting is an issue which plagues many of those responsible for the direction of Intelligence efforts. In some ways there is an analogy between this problem and a question which faces universities today. Current Intelligence work can be equated with teaching, while long-term studies equate with research. In principle, of course, the two kinds of activity should proceed hand in hand. Without long-term research and the background which this research provides, the knowledge necessary to interpret current events is lacking; without a knowledge of current events longer-term research can quickly become irrelevant.

There is often on the part of the user of Intelligence an understandable preference for the immediately useful data, for specific rather than open-ended opinions and for limited options, and there is some justification for these attitudes. Obviously governments must be aware of current developments which may impinge on the national interest; clearly, Intelligence staffs must be prepared to assist with the day-to-day work of government by answering as accurately and as rapidly as possible the multitude of queries which the policy-makers conjure up each day. Many such queries are quite ephemeral and some are trivial, but a suitable staff must be available to deal with them. Let us suppose as a sample that a report is received that a number of tanks is moving in peacetime to an area from which a threat against some person or place could readily be developed. Some obvious questions must be answered at once. Were the movements overt, or were attempts made to conceal them? Were there any previous indications that such a movement might take place? Had any similar movements taken place previously? Had any movements taken place elsewhere? Was the political situation relevant? Was there any administrative or economic reason for the movement? Could the movement be related to the testing of new weapons? Answers to questions such as these must be provided as rapidly and as comprehensively as possible, but the time spent on such problems must not detract from that devoted to longer-range issues.

Here again Intelligence staffs face a problem, for there exists a certain reluctance to accept informed comment on possible futures as a guide to action. It is widely held, especially in Britain, that attempts to form a view of how the world will look, say, a decade ahead are rarely worth the effort expended on them, and that in any case the 'play of the contingent and the unforeseen' will promptly invalidate any forecasts. I am aware that this is a complicated question and that a good deal of research is now being devoted to methods of long-range forecasting in technological and other fields. My opinion remains that the precise prediction of the timing of an important event is highly unlikely to be possible, especially if the event—an impending coup, for example—is such that secrecy is of importance to the plotters or decision-makers. Further, those responsible for taking major decisions will occasionally act completely out of character; only one or two people thought that Khrushchev would be foolish enough to deploy long-range missiles to Cuba; or that Chamberlain could give a guarantee to Poland in 1939.

These men acted out of character, and there are innumerable other examples of major events which could not in any circumstances have been predicted. On the other hand, Walter Lippman once wrote that prophesy is 'seeing the necessary amongst confusion and insignificance'; and in these limited terms governments and their Intelligence staffs must make the best efforts they can to forecast likely eventualities and courses of events, using such tools as are available for this purpose.

The Intelligence process is not completed by the preparation of an 'end-product'—a current Intelligence report or an Intelligence estimate. There still remain what Allen Dulles considered the major problems of ensuring that the product is still relevant and reaches the right user at the right moment, that it is presented convincingly and that the user pays attention to it. Here is raised the delicate and subtle question of the relationship of the Intelligence officer to the policy-maker, an issue I have touched on in earlier chapters.

The fact must be faced that the chief rival of the Intelligence end-product in the mind of the policy-maker is the policy-maker's own experience, and the information available to him from other non-Intelligence sources. This information often consists of no more than hearsay or press reports, which are attractively packaged and sometimes easier to read than official documents. The problem is compounded by the fact that the growth of communications has led to the creation of a group of commentators whose claim to knowledge of political and military affairs is only too frequently equalled by their ignorance. These pundits are convincing before the event, but an analysis of their statements often makes obvious their lack of basic factual data and the shallowness of their arguments. There has in recent years been a considerable amount of discussion in the United States on 'managed' news, but I cannot help feeling that there is often a great deal to be gained from ensuring that public opinion is briefed as fully as possible from official sources. I cannot see why, within the limits imposed by security, the Intelligence authorities should not take a hand in the game by ensuring that their factual data, which is probably the most accurate, and their estimates, which are probably the most comprehensive and sophisticated, are publicly available in some form or other.

In addition, there appears to persist in the minds of policy-makers a good deal of mistrust about the reliability of Intelligence. There are a number of reasons for this. On occasions in the past the Intelligence product has been of less than the highest quality; sometime the expectations of some policy-makers have been over-optimistic. No Intelligence officer or agency can be right every time, just as no doctor can be infallible in his diagnoses and no lawyer can be certain of the adequacy of his advice on a complex problem. Not even the existence of a first-class Intelligence organization with access to all sources, staffed and trained by the most competent personnel, will guarantee that the right options will be chosen and the right policies pursued. It must, however, be added that there is often an element of intellectual arrogance in the posture of some policy-makers; perhaps a great deal more light should be thrown on the methods by which they arrive at their decisions. The organization and methods of Intelligence have been subject to constant review, but I have often found myself viewing with appalling mistrust many of the generalizations on foreign affairs and foreign countries aired by those responsible for the development of policy.

In practice, of course, a finely balanced co-operative system is vital if Intelligence and policy-making are to be sensibly related. In the first place, the Intelligence input must aim at being of such a consistently high quality as to acquire for itself a reputation for indispensability. Secondly, the policy-maker must ensure that the Intelligence staffs receive as much help as is possible in establishing their priorities, so that the bulk of their work will be relevant. In this way situations such as some I remember during World War II can perhaps be avoided. On one occasion I found a large staff assembling immense detail about the island of Corsica long after the decision had been reached that the island should not be an objective of a major Allied attack. In another case air photograph interpreters were found to be examining and reporting on German railroads as military targets long after our advancing troops had captured the areas they were studying. To solve such problems satisfactorily it is necessary continuously to develop contacts between the Intelligence authorities and the policy-makers, so that the relevant questions are asked and appropriate answers provided in a timely and coherent fashion.

As Gauché found to his cost, no Intelligence estimate can compensate for a lack of national will to take action or, in a military context, for an absence of reserves at a crucial moment. Neither can even the best Intelligence estimate be a substitute for political judgement.

The best example of a senior Intelligence officer faced with this kind of dilemma was John McCone, when he realized that a policy was being considered for Vietnam which was contrary to his Intelligence estimates. He made his protest, and he did all he could to ensure that what he considered a policy blunder would not be made because of a lack of Intelligence. The Intelligence officer must not obtrude too far into the policy deliberations, but he must be prepared to dispose immediately of any argument that appears to be based on a distortion of the known facts. He must also be careful to ensure that the Intelligence staffs cannot be accused of error if the policy fails. He cannot do this, however, unless he is present when policy is discussed.

In spite of the efficiency of the Intelligence organization of the United States, some of their Intelligence still fails to carry conviction. In his report on the Vietnam war published in 1968, General Westmoreland, the United States commander, admitted that he did not appreciate the true nature and scope of the widespread communist Tet offensive of 1967, despite strong Intelligence warnings that such attacks might well take place. He then added, 'It did not occur to us that the enemy would undertake suicidal attacks in the face of our power—and he did just that.' Reading between the lines of the report, it appears that Intelligence warnings were ignored in favour of the intuitive feelings of operational staffs.

This brings me to the one further point with which I wish to deal before tackling the more complex subjects of Intelligence organization and personnel. This is the question of the criticism which any Intelligence organization or agency must invariably face. In spite of current misapprehensions, Intelligence activities as practised in the West are not evil or immoral; they are not undemocratic; nor are they breeding grounds for conspiracies or attempts at 'invisible' or secret government. In the present state of the world no nation which aspires to the protection of itself and its interests dares be without an Intelligence apparatus.

I suppose that the mass of current criticism arises from ignorance of the functions and responsibilities of an Intelligence organization. Intelligence, I repeat, is the acquisition, collation and evaluation of information which is needed for policy- and decision-making, and a great deal of this activity is overt and hardly to be differentiated from the more obvious forms of research.

Possibly some of the disrespect into which the Intelligence function has fallen arises from its passion for secrecy, a point which Cavendish-Bentinck was quick to recognize. Clearly, certain parts of an Intelligence organization are of more sensitivity than others, but this is also true of many commercial enterprises. Certainly, there are some areas and details which it would not be in the national interest to expose to public gaze, and thus to the potential enemy. One obvious example is sources of information; many, as I have said, are quite overt, but some sources, both human and technical, are of such a character that their continued success depends upon the opponent remaining in ignorance either of their employment or certainly of the success being achieved. In these cases, there is no alternative to secrecy.

The analogies between national Intelligence agencies, university research departments and national research organizations such as the RAND Corporation in the United States are revealing. For example, many of the most important published books on strategy and defence economics have been written at RAND or have been based upon work done at RAND. Although naturally no classified information has been published in these works, the authors' knowledge of secret matters in the fields of international affairs and national security policy has clearly been of assistance to them, in that it has prevented them from perpetuating those distortions of the real situation which are so often apparent in the work of writers and journalists who operate completely outside the government environment. Unpalatable as it may be to some, there are areas, and important areas, in which the totality of information on a given subject is available only to governments, and those without access to this information are likely to arrive at wrong conclusions, or at least to work at a considerable disadvantage.

Perhaps the ideal agency would be one which prepared 'all-source' classified estimates and appreciations for its government, but made available as much information as possible on given subjects for more general consumption. At the very least, the standard of public and parliamentary debate on many of the complex issues that face the modern world might be immeasurably improved.

Finally, if the Intelligence community is afraid of criticism, I can only advise it to issue gloomy forecasts! It is my experience that the situation of the Intelligence estimator is not unlike that of the stock market analyst and forecaster. Cheerful forecasts are bitterly resented if they turn out to be wrong, and forgotten if they are correct. Gloomy forecasts on the other hand are forgotten if they are wrong because everyone is relieved that the worst has not happened. Consistently gloomy forecasting can therefore bring a reputation for great wisdom. The good Intelligence man, however, is less concerned with his reputation for infallibility than with the integrity of his judgement, whether it happens to give rise to serious concern or removes a spurious threat.

*

The details and composition of any national Intelligence organization will inevitably be determined by personalities and by a country's internal and external preoccupations. The governmental structures of most developed countries include a variety of independent agencies or departments concerned in one way or another with Intelligence. The main organizational problem is the extent to which these should be under or independent of central direction and control. The extreme of decentralization would be for each to set its own priorities, to receive raw Intelligence material direct from its sources, and to make its own arrangements for collation and analysis on the subjects with which it is concerned. This is very nearly the situation that obtained in Britain between the wars; it was nearly disastrous then, and it would be much more likely to be disastrous now. Intelligence information can no longer be spread amongst recipients in accordance with simple rules. The problems are now much too complex for an arrangement of this kind; social, economic, scientific, technological, military and political moves and responses act and react on each other. An evaluator or estimator in any field must have access to information on developments in all other fields if his appreciations are to be realistic.

The independent position of the CIA was the result of a conscious decision that the President and his advisers should, if they wished, be able to obtain a view of situations that was independent of the traditional departments of government, and it was accepted that this arrangement would create tensions with other departments. In other countries proud and ancient departments of state may be less prepared to contemplate changes of these kinds. There are interests which resent changes in the status quo, and many who would react strongly against any attempt to interfere with their areas of alleged expertise or to inject Intelligence assessments at cabinet level with no previous filtering by departmental officials.

Nevertheless, it is my belief that as Britain's political and military resources contract in relative terms, its need for an independent and centrally controlled Intelligence community organized on modern lines will grow. Generally, when resources are limited extra care must be taken to ensure that they are deployed to the best advantage. Within the Intelligence community itself, too, it becomes more and more necessary to ensure that priorities reflect actual national needs and aspirations. It does not add to national prestige or effectiveness to accumulate masses of information on subjects on which no action is possible. What is necessary is to make the right decisions concerning areas of interest, and to study these areas competently.

I do not think that such an organization need be unwieldy or excessively costly, as long as the necessary element of centralized control is firmly established, and as long as the staff is competent and professional.

It is important that those who direct the Intelligence effort in senior positions should be independent of any department and have a broad knowledge of affairs if judgement is to be objective, and affected neither consciously or unconsciously by the wish to see some particular policy followed. Strong and narrow political convictions can only tend to interfere with objectivity; it is unlikely for example that an individual with an anti-American bias will be able to make an impartial judgement upon questions concerned with the Vietnam war; nor can someone with very strong anti-communist beliefs be depended upon to pronounce impartially upon Soviet motives and intentions. Prejudices such as these can assume extraordinary importance; it is surprising how simple it is, once an initial erroneous judgement has been made, to fit new information into the framework suggested by a preconceived idea.

It is understandably difficult to find such paragons, and to persuade them to accept senior appointments within an Intelligence community. At lower levels, where the rewards and prestige are less, and sometimes, Treasuries being what they are, considerably less, the problem is even more difficult. Let us first consider officers of the armed forces, who are naturally in the preponderance in Military Intelligence agencies and play important roles in national agencies. At one time a general belief existed that an appointment to the Intelligence community would almost inevitably constitute a bar to further promotion, and that their professional knowledge of their own service will be degraded by an absorption in the affairs of foreign countries. An officer who spent much time as an attaché, or for that matter in an Intelligence directorate or staff appointment, was not generally highly regarded in his own service. These attitudes have been proved to be ridiculous, and they are changing. When I returned after many years in Intelligence to command an infantry battalion and found British methods vastly out-of-date compared with those I had observed in Germany, I was able to make use of my experience abroad to improve the training of my battalion. Similarly, General Gauché, the head of the French Deuxième Bureau, relates that when between the wars he returned for periods of duty with French troops he constantly found himself making comparisons between French and foreign military training and applying his knowledge of the latter to the improvement of the former.

In the German Army the situation was somewhat better. Service in the Intelligence community was not wholly detrimental to a successful military career, although this was largely due to the fact that in pre-1914 days it was the practice for up-and-coming young staff officers to made a tour of duty in Intelligence. Ulrich Liss of Foreign Armies West maintained that an appointment on an Intelligence staff was the most rewarding of any position open to a serving officer. I think he was right. Service in Intelligence can vastly enlarge the sometimes limited horizons of many military officers, and introduce them—albeit perhaps somewhat superficially—to the complexities of international relations, economics and science.

Nevertheless, I continue to regard it as vital that a serving officer should return at intervals from Intelligence appointments to serve with troops. Only in this way can he maintain his professional competence and, perhaps more important, maintain some contact with the 'real' military world, to the support of which Military Intelligence efforts are in the end devoted.

However knowledgeable service officers may be in military matters, the core of any national Intelligence community, even in the military sub-divisions, must be primarily civilian, for only by employing civilians as career Intelligence officers can long-term continuity and professionalism be established. In a modern Intelligence structure there

is a requirement for specialized expertise in areas of economics, socio-
logy, science and technology which can only be met by the employment of civilians on a fully professional basis.

The recruitment of suitable civilians remains a difficult task. The
current climate of opinion amongst young graduates cannot be said
to be very warmly disposed towards a career in what many would
regard as a nationalistic or even militaristic environment, or in an area
which has overtones of secrecy or concealment. Nevertheless if the
organization is to be effective it must rely heavily on able young men,
who perhaps have fewer preconceptions about the world than their
elders. On the other hand, many young political or social scientists
tend to view the modern scene over-critically. Recruitment tends to be
confined to apparently 'safe' circles, and the machine is denied brilliance and imagination which might have contributed to its work.

Apart from such considerations, it remains true that Intelligence
work has many frustrations. As we have seen, any mistake is likely to
find ready public criticism, to which it is often hard or impossible to
make any effective reply, either by reference to the real facts of the
case at issue, or by comment on previous successes. In Intelligence, the
balance sheet can never be finely drawn, especially in public, and the
dividends paid can never be openly declared.

On the other hand, given a reasonable career structure and rewards
more or less comparable with those available in other fields, the
satisfactions to be obtained from Intelligence work are often great.
Intelligence is, or should be, at the heart of affairs, and Intelligence
officers are increasingly in a position to participate in important policies
and decisions. Further, the Intelligence world is essentially interdiscip-
linary. The economist must take political and technical factors into
account; the scientists must judge possible developments with one eye
upon their economic impact; the academic researcher finds himself in
touch with the practical and pragmatic policy-maker. Attractions of
these kinds should surely make it possible to recruit a fair proportion
of available first-class brains. I would go further and say that a central
Intelligence agency should be able to pick recruits from civil servants
with appropriate qualifications and that they should be made available
by their parent departments and guaranteed that there will be no loss
of salary or promotion prospects because of this.

Provision should be made for recruitment at appropriate grades of older men and women who have served in other walks of life, in journalism perhaps or in business or banking, or in universities; perhaps even some persons with experience of policy-making could be induced to join Intelligence staffs. Some way must be found by which new graduates and experienced persons can be combined in an organization without detriment to the careers of either group. In addition, as in many similar organizations, arrangements must be made to permit brilliant analysts to reach the higher levels of the career structure without having to asume overwhelming administrative responsibilities.

It seems especially difficult to choose the right scientists and economists for Intelligence duties. Experimental scientists, for example, tend to devise artificial situations which may never occur in the real world, and their conclusions are heavily dependent upon the results of experiments with these situations. This is as if an Intelligence officer were able to rearrange the dispositions of the enemy's forces in order to discover the results of the battle. On the other hand, the observational scientists—the astronomers, geologists, synoptic meteorologists—cannot alter the situations they study, but are passive observers of nature. Like Intelligence officers they have to draw their conclusions from observations of the real world—observations which are sometimes fragmentary and often confusing.

Similar problems attend the choice of economists. In general terms, the economist believes that any problem can be quantified, and has great confidence that he can make a reasonable prediction on the basis of mathematical extrapolation. This optimism is often proved to be unjustified, even when the predictions are about one's own country on the basis of complete information. Statistical and other material on foreign countries, and especially on our most important potential enemies, is rarely complete, and the economist who tends to see all problems in quantitative terms is at a loss.

For these and other reasons, the history of economic Intelligence contains many examples of forecasts that were quite wrong. It was estimated for example that the bombing of the ball-bearings plant at Schweinfurt in Germany in World War II, which was carried out in daylight and with great accuracy by the United States Air Force, would have a considerable effect on German armaments production. The Germans proved that it was possible to employ less sophisticated bearings for a wide range of uses, and by reconstructing plants with surprising rapidity. It would be wrong to suggest that there have been no important gains in expertise over the past quarter of a century. New errors will certainly be made, but some of the earlier mistakes are avoided by those with long professional memories.

It seems to me important that the economist employed on Intelligence duties should act as a member of a team. He may demand that the social scientist should relate his theories to economic possibilities and that the military officer should recognize economic realities in estimating future military capabilities, but he should not assume that he alone is able to predict economic developments. There seem to be few limits either to the exploitation of substitute materials, or to the proverbial tightening of belts. An experienced wartime planner, who was also an economist, once suggested that the most important contribution to practical affairs that the economist could offer rested 'not so much on the strength of his own more esoteric learning but rather on the strength of the more elementary platitudes on the subject'.

*

The Intelligence process—the collection of information, its collation and evaluation, and the communication of the end-product to the appropriate user at the right time—is as applicable in the world of business and commerce as it is in government. This becomes increasingly true as business becomes international in character, and its requirements become similar to those of governments. Ultimately, effective business depends upon accurate decision-making, and it seems that it could with advantage adopt some of the Intelligence techniques which have been developed by government. Many of the more constructive aspects of Intelligence work and the concepts which underlie them are especially worth the attention of those parts of the business world concerned with export trade and overseas investment. It should eventually be possible to create in business those conditions which will allow the higher management to make decisions on a broader base of knowledge and information than has sometimes been possible in the past; leaders in commerce and industry can no longer pretend that the world is confined to their balance sheets, and divorce their decisions from events in the world around them.

Almost all the information required in business or commerce can be obtained overtly. Sources are many and varied: many corporations have their own representatives overseas; all have access to government departments of one kind or another which make available information on a wide variety of commercial subjects although there is much need to see that it is selective and relevant; there are books, trade and technical periodicals, the press, government statistics, and so on—as well as innumerable private and semi-private organizations and agencies which make it their business to disseminate information, usually for a fee.

In recent years the commercial activities of embassies have increased in importance and become considerably more effective and their staffs more accessible to the business world. Personal contact with industry and industrial leaders have led, on the one hand, to a greater understanding by members of the diplomatic service of the capabilities and problems of industry and, on the other, to a greater appreciation by industry of the kinds of assistance that can reasonably be expected from the service.

This process has not yet gone far enough in Britain, where the future lies less in political initiatives and more in commercial success. I would like to see the commercial representation at all major British embassies considerably increased at the expense of the political representatives. At the very least, the Ambassador's deputy should be a commercially trained officer, possibly seconded from the world of commerce itself. Further, these commercial representatives must be guided by priorities, and some system must be established whereby British business is able to influence these priorities, so that reporting from overseas becomes more rapidly responsive to commercial requirements.

The mere acquisition of information is, however, not enough, and each business must take the necessary organizational steps within itself to ensure that the information it receives is collated, evaluated and presented to its own decision-makers, possibly by a small group independent of the normal salary and promotion structure reporting directly to the chairman or managing director. It is here that the implications of the main difference between business and government begin to show themselves. Business must always be conscious of the cost-benefit relationship; in other words, although it may be inconvenient for a government agency to be flooded with irrelevant or useless information, this is not in itself disastrous. In business, on the other hand, the costs of handling, reading and filing this information must be borne in mind, and a serious effort made to determine whether the additional returns that arise from possession of the information total more than it costs. It is very doubtful whether this cost-benefit ratio is quantifiable, and its value can probably only be judged by those who have a view of the total progress of a given enterprise over a long period of trial and error. But above all, any suggestion such as I have made must be so introduced that they speed, not hinder decisions.

Earlier in this chapter I commented that in a relatively limited environment the spy could well have a role to play. The world of business and commerce is such an area, and there is evidence that the activities of agents in this field is a growing threat to the even tenor of commercial operations. There is an increasing tendency to institutionalize this process of acquiring data, and to seek information with considerably more formality and perhaps with the assistance of a third party. This third party may well be a professional industrial espionage agency, a number of which are said to exist in the United States and some of which may exist in Britain and other countries. The methods such professional industrial spies employ are time-honoured: waste-paper baskets are searched; the lives and habits of competitor's employees are systematically investigated; employees are socially cultivated and unknowingly interrogated; bribery and blackmail are not unknown; occasionally use is made of sophisticated equipment to tap telephones or eavesdrop on conversations or meetings. The opponent or competitor is out to learn all he can about the rival firm's research and financial secrets and to know their plan for marketing and sales. Documents and people rather than 'bugging' devices are probably his two best sources of information. In these days of take-over bids and company acquisitions, a spy who can reconstruct the profit and loss account of an intended victim, or provide a list of major shareholders with notes on their likely sympathies in the event of a bid, has valuable information for sale.

It seems to me important to judge the extent to which complex counter-measures against industrial espionage are worth their cost in time and money and human relations. Unless they are vital, as in the case of some state secrets, security measures can sometimes be self-defeating either because they tend to interfere with the normal working of an organization or because they interrupt those channels of communication which are important to the success of any enterprise. There is a further important consideration. Too great an emphasis on security may well have a detrimental effect on employer-employee relations since few activities are more likely to destroy good industrial relations and promote suspicion—and this at a time when it is important that management and labour should understand and have confidence in each other. Generally, I think it must be accepted that employees whose livelihood depends upon the continued prosperity of the firm they work for will, if they are made aware of the dangers of indiscretion, themselves take such steps as are necessary to preserve the security of the company's operations. It is important for executives to bear in mind the possibility of industrial espionage, but the best remedies and precautions seem to me to be those dictated by common sense. Thus in industry or commerce, only men of the highest discretion and balanced judgement should be allowed to handle these problems if they are to be kept in their proper perspective. One of the most successful security officers I knew in World War II was Colonel (later Sir Brian) Mountain, who brought to his work not only previous experience in the armed services but a vast knowledge of human relations acquired as a leading business executive. Executives may console themselves somewhat with the thought that the products of the greatest spies in the political and military fields have not always been either relevant or accurate; there is little reason why the industrial spy should fare much better.

★

Over the centuries, the political or military leader has always found a need for what we now call Intelligence. As long ago as the sixth century B.C., Sun Tzu, the Chinese military theorist, wrote in *On the Art of War*, 'What enables the wise sovereign and the good general to strike and conquer and achieve things beyond the reach of ordinary men is foreknowledge.' The truth is that, given relatively even capabilities, he who possesses the best and most accurate information at the moment of decision will usually win, whether the battle be political, military or commercial; what is more, information better than that available to an opponent will often compensate for lesser capabilities.

An important lesson that emerges from an examination of the

actions and reactions of men of Intelligence from Hentsch in 1914 to McCone in 1967 is that Intelligence officers must be prepared to fight to gain acceptance for their ideas. When they have something of striking importance to impart or when they seek to bring to notice some significant new trend, their views will in the nature of things be ahead of the run of common acceptance; nearly all our men of Intelligence had to undertake metaphorical struggles of this kind. A second and related point is that none of them managed to achieve a completely ideal relationship with his policy-makers. If Hentsch had been better informed of the true state of the German forces in 1914, it is doubtful whether he would have made the drastic decision to retreat. If Gauché in March 1935 had been able to exert greater influence on his High Command, there is a possibility that the last opportunity to stop Hitler would not have been lost; it is conceivable that, if there had been any sign of French resistance, the German General Staff might have been able to dissuade Hitler from further adventures. If Liss had been better informed of the plans for attacking France in 1940, there is little doubt that the German advance would have proceeded even more smoothly than it did, for Intelligence reports would have dissipated early fears of French flank attacks on the Panzer columns breaking through in the Ardennes. And if Kennedy and his successor had listened to McCone more carefully and given greater weight to his estimates, the United States might not have become involved in its fruitless dilemma in Vietnam.

A third lesson is that Intelligence is indivisible. No area of activity—politics, economics, military affairs, science and technology—can be regarded as a subject apart and treated in isolation; for this reason there must be central control and direction of all Intelligence activities by a chief who should have personal access to the top policy and decision-makers in his own government, that is to the Head of State, the President or the Prime Minister. Fourthly, Intelligence must not strive for perfection at the expense of timeliness. In 1955 the Hoover Commission in the United States reached the conclusion that Intelligence dealt with all those things which should be known in advance of initiating a course of action. Such a definition contains within itself the seeds of misunderstanding. Consider, for example, an archaeologist who continues to dig for ever in the hope of finding a final piece of evidence which will confirm his theory and complete his picture; if it never turns up, his work is wasted. The Intelligence estimator must at an appropriate moment stop, and report his conclusions on the basis of the evidence that is at that moment available. Similarly, the policy-maker must not delay his decision too long in the hope that missing Intelligence will be acquired. Intelligence pictures are rarely, if ever, complete.

Fifthly, secrecy must not be overemphasized. The requirement for secrecy must be weighed against the disadvantages that are likely to arise from limited circulation of a piece of information. The fact that Intelligence is meant to be used must always be in the forefront of the Intelligence officer's mind, and he must make every effort to ensure that his information and estimates are disseminated as widely as possible.

I have had direct and indirect experience of the Intelligence machines of four countries: Britain, the United States, France and Germany. Between the wars there was to my mind no doubt of the professional competence of the French and German Intelligence structures, although their products were not always used to the best advantage. During World War II, British Intelligence came to fulfilment, and clearly led the world, especially in its technical achievements in radio-interception. Since then, the United States, basing itself partly on British experience, has grown to pre-eminence. The American collection effort and the Washington machinery for control and co-ordination of the massive apparatus of United States Intelligence will not easily be surpassed. Gradually the Intelligence machinery has become an essential part of government; official announcements demonstrate that very few important decisions are taken without the views of the Director of Central Intelligence being taken into account. Cavendish-Bentinck went far to solve the problem of closer co-operation with the planners by becoming an adviser to them while at the same time retaining chairmanship of the Joint Intelligence Committee.

Britain continues to produce competent analyses, although she cannot compete in the more recondite collection efforts, nor allot such a wealth of resources to collation and evaluation; further, the British effort suffers in comparison with the American because Britain is not so closely involved in the main technological problems of the age. One of Britain's most important continuing failures, however, seems to me to lie in a reluctance to accept that the Intelligence product must be the work of professionals and constitutes a vital factor to decision-making. National character has a good deal to do with this; too often in Britain a policy-maker—or in business a chief executive—has felt himself competent to choose the facts, interpret them and make the decisions. I have found a depressing inclination to prefer lunchtime rumour to considered estimates, and preconceived notions to argued cases. These problems of acceptance will never be solved until the Intelligence machine can not only produce a convincing product, but also be so organized and controlled that it can take aggressive steps to get it accepted.

BIBLIOGRAPHY

Abel, Elie: *The Missile Crisis*. Philadelphia, Lippincott, 1966.

Asprey, Robert B.: *The First Battle of the Marne*. Philadelphia, Lippincott, 1962.

Barclay, C. N.: *Armistice 1918*. London, Dent, 1968; New York, A. S. Barnes, 1969.

Barnett, Correlli: *The Swordbearers: Studies in Supreme Command in the First World War*. London, Eyre & Spottiswoode, 1963; New York, Morrow, 1963.

Beaufre, General André: *1940: The Fall of France*. London, Cassell, 1967; New York, Knopf, 1968.

Blond, Georges: *The Marne* (trans. H. Eaton Hart). London, Macdonald, 1962; New York, Stackpole, 1966.

Chapman, Guy, O.B.E., M.C.: *Why France Collapsed*. London, Cassell, 1968; as *Why France Fell: The Defeat of the French Army in 1940*. New York, Holt, Rinehart & Winston, 1969.

Charteris, Brigadier-General John, C.M.G., D.S.O.: *Field Marshal Lord Haig*. London, Cassell, 1929.

— *At G.H.Q.* London, Cassell, 1931.

Churchill, Winston S.: *The Second World War* (6 vols.). London, Cassell, 1948–53; Boston, Houghton Mifflin, 1948–54.

Colvin, Ian: *Chief of Intelligence*. London, Gollancz, 1951.

Dulles, Allen (ed.): *Great True Spy Stories*. A Giniger Book, New York, Harper & Row, 1968; London, Collins, 1969.

— *The Craft of Intelligence*. A Giniger Book. New York, Harper & Row, 1963; London, Weidenfeld & Nicolson, 1964.

von Einem, Generaloberst Karl: *Ein Armeeführer erlebt den Weltkrieg*. Leipzig, Hase & Koehlar, 1938.

— *Errinerung – eines Soldaten*. Leipzig, Koehler, 1933.

Edmonds, Brigadier-General Sir James E., C.B., C.M.G.: *Military Operations, France and Belgium, 1915* (Official History of the Great War). London, Macmillan, 1928.

Erzberger, Mathias: *Erlebnisse im Weltkrieg*. Stuttgart, Deutsche-Verlags-Anstalt, 1920.

Gauché, General: *Le Deuxième Bureau au Travail, 1935–1940*. Paris, Amiot-Dumont, 1953.

de Gaulle, General Charles: *La France et son Armée*. Paris, Berger–Levrault, 1945.

Gleichen, Major-General Lord Edward: *A Guardsman's Memories*. Edinburgh, Blackwood, 1932.

Haig, Field-Marshal Lord: *The Private Papers of Douglas Haig, 1914–1919* (ed. Robert Blake). London, Eyre & Spottiswoode, 1952; New York, Verry, 1952.

Horne, Alistair: *To Lose a Battle; France, 1940.* London, Macmillan, 1969; Boston, Little, Brown, 1969.

Keitel, Wilhelm: *The Memoirs of Field-Marshal Keitel* (ed. Walter Görlitz). London, Kimber, 1965; New York, Stein & Day, 1966.

Leverkuehn, Paul: *German Military Intelligence* (trans. R. H. Stevens and Constantine FitzGibbon). London, Weidenfeld & Nicolson, 1954.

Liddell Hart, Captain B. H.: *The Other Side of the Hill*. Enlarged edition. London, Cassell, 1951.

— *Memoirs*. London, Cassell, 1965 (2 vols.); Putnam's, New York, 1965 (1 vol.).

Liss, General Ulrich: *Westfront, 1939–1940*. Neckargemund, K. Vowinckel, 1959. (*And various articles by General Liss.*)

von Manstein, Field-Marshal Erich: *Verlorene Siege*. Bonn, Atheneum, 1955.

— *Aus Einem Soldatenleben*. Bonn, Athenäum, 1958.

McLachlan, Donald: *Room 39*. London, Weidenfeld & Nicolson, 1968; New York, Athenäum, 1968.

Murphy, Robert: *Diplomat Among the Warriors*. New York, Doubleday, 1964; London, Collins, 1964.

Nicolai, Colonel W.: *The German Secret Service* (trans. George Renwick). London, Stanley Paul, 1924.

— *Nachrichtendienst, Presse und Volkstimmung in Weltkrieg*. Berlin, Mittler, 1920.

Nicolson, Hon Sir Harold: *The Congress of Vienna*. London, Constable, 1946; New York, Viking.

Paget, R. T., K.C., M.P.: *Manstein, His Campaigns and His Trial*. London, Collins, 1951.

Ransom, H. H.: *Central Intelligence and National Security*. Cambridge, Mass., Harvard University Press, 1958.

Ropp, Theodore: *War in the Modern World*. Durham, N.C., Duke University Press, 1959.

Stehlin, General Paul: *Témoignage pour l'histoire*. Paris, Laffont, 1964.

Strong, Sir Kenneth, K.B.E., C.B.: *Intelligence at the Top: Recollections of an Intelligence Officer*. A Giniger Book. London, Cassell, 1968; New York, Doubleday, 1969.

Tedder, Marshal of the R.A.F. Lord, G.C.B.: *With Prejudice*. Cassell London, 1966; Boston, Little, Brown, 1967.

Terraine, John: *Douglas Haig: The Educated Soldier*. London, Hutchinson, 1963.

von Tippelskirch, General Kurt: *Geschichte des Zweiten Weltkriegs*. Bonn, Athenäum, 1954.

Tuchman, Barbara W.: *August 1914*. New York, Macmillan; London, Constable, 1962.

Warlimont, General W.: *Inside Hitler's Headquarters, 1939-1945* (trans. R. H. Barry). London, Weidenfeld & Nicolson, 1964; New York, Praeger, 1964.

Weintal, E., and Bartlett, C.: *Facing the Brink*. New York, Charles Scribner's Sons, 1967; London, Hutchinson, 1967.

Wemyss, Admiral of the Fleet Lord Wester-: *Life and Letters* (ed. Lady Wester-Wemyss). London, Eyre & Spottiswoode, 1935.

Wheeler-Bennett, Sir John: *Brest-Litovsk: the Forgotten Peace*. London, Macmillan, 1938; New York, Macmillan.

— *The Nemesis of Power: the German Army in Politics, 1918-1945*. London, Macmillan, 1954; New York, St. Martin's Press.

Wilmot, Chester: *The Struggle for Europe* (new edition). London, Collins, 1965; New York, Harper & Row, 1965.

I would like to express my thanks to the authors and publishers concerned for permission to make short quotations for some of the books listed above.

K. S.

INDEX

INDEX

Abwehr (German Secret Service), 65–69, 91, 95
Albrecht of Wurttemberg, Duke, 13n, 19
Albert Canal, 83, 84
Alliance for Progress, 137
American Intelligence, see CIA
Anspach case, 143
Arab States, 133
Ardennes, 58, 82, 83–4; Battle of (1945), 61, 131, 168
Arlon gap, 58
armistice negotiations: French (1940), 97–8, 103–7; German (1918), 96, 98–102, (1945), 96, 97, 101, 104, 108–10; Italian (1943), 108, 109, 110; Russian (1917), 102–3.
'Army of Intervention in Belgium' (French), 84
Atomic Energy Commission, United States, 136, 148
Austria, annexation by Germany, 43, 46, 50, 75
Austria-Hungary, 7, 12

Badini, Count, 50
'Barbarossa', Operation, 91–4
Baril, Colonel, 57
Bay of Pigs episode, 130–1, 135, 136
Beaufre, General, 40, 147
Beck, General, 62, 125
Bedell Smith, General, 109, 131; as head of CIA, 126, 127–8, 141
Belgian Army, 12, 14, 80, 82, 83
Belgium, 4, 12, 13, 14; and World War II, 54, 59, 61, 76, 79–80, 82–4, 87
Berlin, 46, 48, 50, 53, 78, 100, 101, 109

Bethmann-Hollweg, Theobald von, 4, 9
Blackshirts, 75
Blitzkrieg, 43
Blomberg, Field-Marshal von, 24–5, 74
BND (Intelligence organization of Federal German Republic), 91
Bohemia, 52
Bradley, General Omar, 24, 122
'Brandenburgers', 66
Brauchitsch, Field-Marshal von, 75, 80; and 1940 armistice, 103, 107
Brest-Litovsk, Treaty of, 102–3
British Army: Intelligence in World War I, 26–34; in Rhineland, 38, 64, 87
British Expeditionary Force: in World War I, 14, 16, 26, 31; in World War II, 57
British GHQ, in World War I, 26–8
British Intelligence, 111–23; in World War I, 26–34; from 1939–45, 113–123; and events in Germany, 112–15, 118–23; lack of co-ordination, 113–15; and Norwegian campaign, 114–15; obsession with secrecy, 114–15, 122; leadership given by Cavendish-Bentinck, 115–23
Brooke, Field-Marshal Sir Alan (later Lord Alanbrooke), 119–20
Brownshirts, 44, 64, 65
Brussels, 80, 82
Bulge, Battle of the (Ardennes, 1945), 61, 131, 168
Bülow, General (later Field-Marshal) Karl von, 13; and retreat from Marne, 15, 16, 17–18, 21

177